IMAGES
of America

PITTSBURGH
1758–2008

On the cover: Here is the evening rush of traffic as it flows over the Liberty Bridge crossing the Monongahela River in August 1951. (Clyde Hare.)

IMAGES
of America

PITTSBURGH
1758–2008

Pittsburgh Post-Gazette and
Carnegie Library of Pittsburgh

Copyright © 2008 by Pittsburgh Post-Gazette and Carnegie Library of Pittsburgh
ISBN 978-1-5316-4103-0

Published by Arcadia Publishing
Charleston, South Caorlina

Library of Congress Catalog Card Number: 2008926675

For all general information contact Arcadia Publishing at:
Telephone 843-853-2070
Fax 843-853-0044
E-mail sales@arcadiapublishing.com
For customer service and orders:
Toll-Free 1-888-313-2665

Visit us on the Internet at www.arcadiapublishing.com

To all the Pittsburghers who came by wagons over the mountains,
who worked long hours in hot mills,
who scrubbed laundry and floors to keep their families together,
who worked for clean air and greener buildings,
who strove to make their place a better place.

CONTENTS

Acknowledgments		6
Introduction		7
1.	A Wilderness Fort and Early Settlement: 1758–1815	9
2.	A City's First Steps, Then Disaster: 1816–1845	15
3.	Pittsburgh Rebuilds and Expands: 1846–1859	21
4.	The Civil War and the Iron City: 1860–1879	31
5.	The Gilded Age of Industry: 1880–1899	43
6.	A New Century, a World War: 1900–1919	51
7.	A Skyscraper University Grows in Oakland: 1920–1939	69
8.	Another World War and a Renaissance: 1940–1959	77
9.	Civil Unrest and Title Teams: 1960–1979	93
10.	Big Steel Falls, High-Tech Rises: 1980–2008	111

ACKNOWLEDGMENTS

Pittsburgh: 1758–2008 commemorates the 250th anniversary of the founding of "Pittsborough" at the forks of the Ohio River. This book owes a debt of gratitude to the authors of *A Pittsburgh Album*, which the Post-Gazette first published in 1959 to commemorate the city's bicentennial. Researched and written by Roy Stryker, founder of the Pittsburgh Photographic Library, and Post-Gazette reporter Mel Seidenberg, it drew heavily on the archives of Carnegie Library of Pittsburgh, the Pittsburgh Photographic Library, and the Post-Gazette's own "morgue" of news photographs. Subsequent editions in 1976 and 1986 were supplemented by the Post-Gazette's Gerald Patterson with new material from the Post-Gazette archives. With this edition, special recognition goes to Patricia Lowry for her ability to capture 250 years of Pittsburgh history with an extraordinary gift for writing, critical eye for accuracy, and grace under pressure.

Two photographs at the end of this book, by Winchester Thurston Upper School students Morgan Gilbreath and Samantha Wanko, are drawn from a juried student photography exhibition with the theme "Imagine What You Can Do Here," sponsored by Carnegie Library of Pittsburgh and the Allegheny County Regional Asset District in honor of the city's 250th birthday.

The names of photographers, when known, or lending institutions appear at the end of captions. Individuals who loaned images for the early chapters of this book have passed on, but their names continue to appear as contributors to honor their memory and generosity.

Images from *A Pittsburgh Album* were selected by Marilyn Cocchiola Holt, Barbara Mistick, Gilbert Pietrzak, and Karlyn Voss at Carnegie Library and, at the Post-Gazette, Angelika Kane, Patricia Lowry, and David Shribman. The manuscript was edited by Angelika Kane, Patricia Lowry, and David Shribman.

Thanks also to John Butler and Larry Roberts for technical support, and to the many Post-Gazette photographers and writers, past and present, whose work appears throughout this book.

INTRODUCTION

The volume you hold in your hands celebrates the past of a city that always has built the future.

Three centuries ago, the British and the French thought they were building future empires at the confluence of the rivers that give shape to our city, to our travel patterns, to our identities. From the Civil War to World War I and World War II, our factories and foundries built the machines and weapons that in turn built dreams of a better world, shorn of slavery and tyranny. They built, too, the tools of peace, of a mass consumer society and a manufacturing superpower that helped build a distinctive American culture at the time of America's greatest international influence. For generations, the shorthand for that has been an intoxicating three-word phrase: the American dream. Here the dreamers worked with iron and steel—and with great imagination, for here not only the manufacturing and commercial arts flourished, but the cultural, medical, and scientific arts flowered as well, and do to this day.

Ours is a city of big, soaring thoughts—how to construct a giant steel complex, how to construct a huge financial empire, how to distribute pickles and ketchup to a worldwide market, how to express genius in the banality of a soup can. But it is also a city of small, enduring gestures—the waving of a simple yellow terry cloth towel on a frigid Sunday afternoon, the simple courtesy of the Pittsburgh left, the beguiling mystery of the french fries in the salad, the way we defy one of our founding nations when we talk of DuBois and North Versailles, the explosion of the senses at the cheese counter at the Strip District store we all call Penn Mac.

Ideas big and small, visions of the past and of the future, the way we celebrate the performances at both Heinz Hall and Heinz Field, the fact that we have a Carnegie Music Hall and a Frick Art Museum all our own—these are the themes of our life, day by day. They are also the themes of our book, page by page. For at the Pittsburgh Post-Gazette, we and our predecessor publications have produced a record of our past and of our dreams of the future, day by day, page by page, for more than two centuries. We are privileged to have you join us in our journey, day by day, page by page.

—David M. Shribman, executive editor, *Pittsburgh Post-Gazette*

We are living history. From Pittsburgh's earliest days, people understood that they could capture history with something as simple as a photograph. For centuries, families have documented their achievements, celebrations, and milestones—as seen through the eyes of a camera lens.

As stewards to our region's diverse history, Carnegie Library of Pittsburgh collects the stories of the people who have helped to shape Pittsburgh. Just as writers record our social history, photographers' observations document the direct social experience. One of our very first photographic collections, shot by Edward S. Curtis, is the most comprehensive work on American Indians. The collection documents tribal lore and culture and, in most cases, is the only recorded history of the American Indian.

Spearheaded in 1950 under the direction of photo documentalist Roy Stryker with a mere 18,000 images, the library's Pittsburgh Photographic Library has preserved much of our own local history. Visual stories captured by Luke Swank, Charles "Teenie" Harris, Regina Fisher, Frank Bingaman, Clyde Hare, Esther Bubley, Abram Brown, Harold Corsini, and others encapsulate the emotion of Pittsburgh's heart and soul—its people. If a picture is worth a thousand words, then the more than 50,000 images that now compose the Pittsburgh Photographic Library speak volumes.

Andrew Carnegie believed in the power of free information. He saw great opportunity in Pittsburgh, a city known for its philanthropy, diverse neighborhoods, and entrepreneurial and industrial spirit. Pittsburgh is also home to the country's public library movement, a legacy that has influenced generations. While the library preserves the past through recorded manuscripts, documents, and artifacts, we also inspire historians, filmmakers, documentalists, and authors who use these items to weave their own tales. As Pittsburgh celebrates its 250th anniversary, we take this opportunity to provide this look at our own rich history.

Pittsburgh is constantly reinventing itself—from the original "Gateway to the West" to a smoky steel town to the incubator for health care, high technology, and education. Just as the city keeps reconfiguring to meet the needs of the times, both as a premier workplace and a center of social life, photographs continue to immortalize the people and neighborhoods that define our region. As we look toward Pittsburgh's vibrant future, we are happy to once again partner with the Pittsburgh Post-Gazette to share with you the story of Pittsburgh through the eyes of its people.

We have a great story to tell!

—Dr. Barbara K. Mistick, president and director, Carnegie Library of Pittsburgh

One

A WILDERNESS FORT AND EARLY SETTLEMENT
1758–1815

Pittsburgh began as a fort at the Forks of the Ohio, on the western frontier. In the 1750s, both the French and the English coveted its strategic location, with easy access to the north and west via the Allegheny, Monongahela, and Ohio Rivers. George Washington, then 21 and a major in the Virginia militia, described its advantages in a letter to Virginia governor Robert Dinwiddie on November 24, 1753:

> As I got down before the Canoe, I spent some Time in viewing the Rivers, and the Land in the Fork; which I think extremely well situated for a Fort, as it has the absolute Command of both Rivers. The Land at the Point is 20 or 25 Feet above the common Surface of the Water; and a considerable Bottom of flat, well-timbered Land all around it, very convenient for Building: The Rivers are each a Quarter of a Mile, or more, across, and run here very near at right Angles: Aligany bearing N. E. and Monongahela S. E. The former of these two is a very rapid and swift running Water; the other deep and still, without any perceptible fall.

In April 1754, Lt. Col. George Washington, at 22, led two Virginia companies into the Great Meadows to try to dislodge the French and their American Indian allies. But rain-filled trenches and, as he wrote, a "constant galding fire upon us" forced his retreat, portrayed here. The following year, he had two horses shot out from under him in the rout of Gen. Edward Braddock's army on the Monongahela plains, where Braddock was killed. It was on the western frontier, now western Pennsylvania, that Washington learned the guerrilla ways of American Indian warfare, how to fight the natives on their own terms, how to placate them with rum and gifts, and ultimately how to defeat them, setting the stage for white settlement. It was in western Pennsylvania that Washington fought for his country—England—against the American Indians and the French, before turning his military skills against the British in the war for independence. (Harper's New Monthly.)

The Marquis Duquesne stirred British colonists to action with a plan to erect military forts from the St. Lawrence to the Mississippi. But failing supply lines from distant bases forced him to stop with the third, Fort Duquesne, a stockade fort at the forks of the Ohio. The French, routed by the British in 1758, destroyed it just before they took flight. (Senator John Heinz History Center.)

England foundered in its attempt to win the New World until the brilliant, aggressive William Pitt the Elder came to power in 1757 as prime minister. His leadership resulted in British victories both in Europe and in the French and Indian War. (Senator John Heinz History Center.)

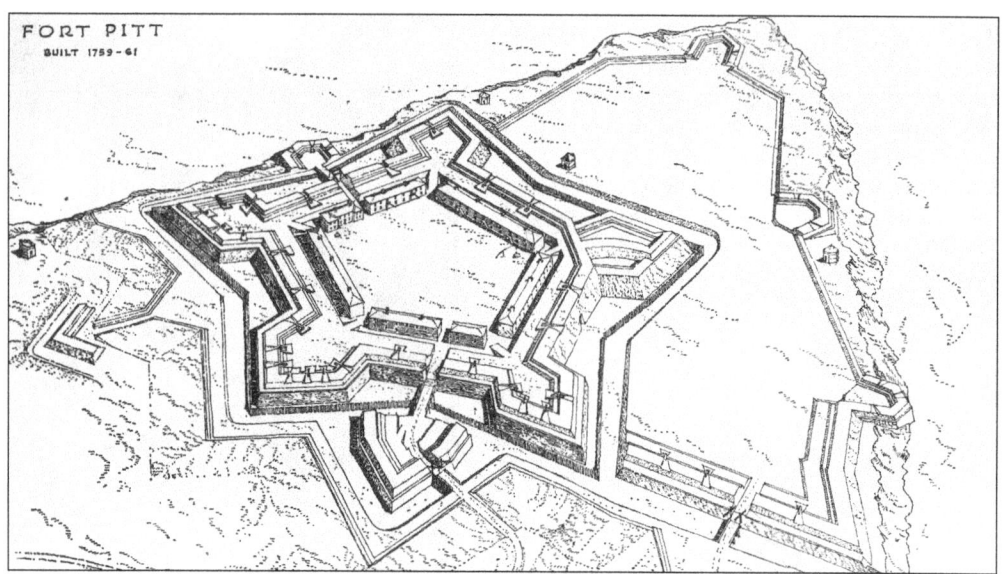

Completed in the winter of 1761, Fort Pitt was the last and largest of the five forts built by the British and the French at the forks of the Ohio as they fought for control of the land. This sketch, drawn by architect and fort historian Charles M. Stotz in the 1950s, shows its brick and earthen ramparts and its outlying redoubts, one of which survives as Pittsburgh's oldest building, the blockhouse of 1764. By 1796, the fort was in ruins; its earthen ramparts were weathering away, and its bricks had been salvaged to build some of the town's earliest houses. (Senator John Heinz History Center.)

Illness compelled British general John Forbes to direct the last six weeks of his victorious march to Fort Duquesne from a litter suspended between two horses. He died in March 1759, almost four months after the British took the forks on November 25, 1758. It was Forbes who named the land at the confluence Pittsborough, in honor of William Pitt. (Senator John Heinz History Center.)

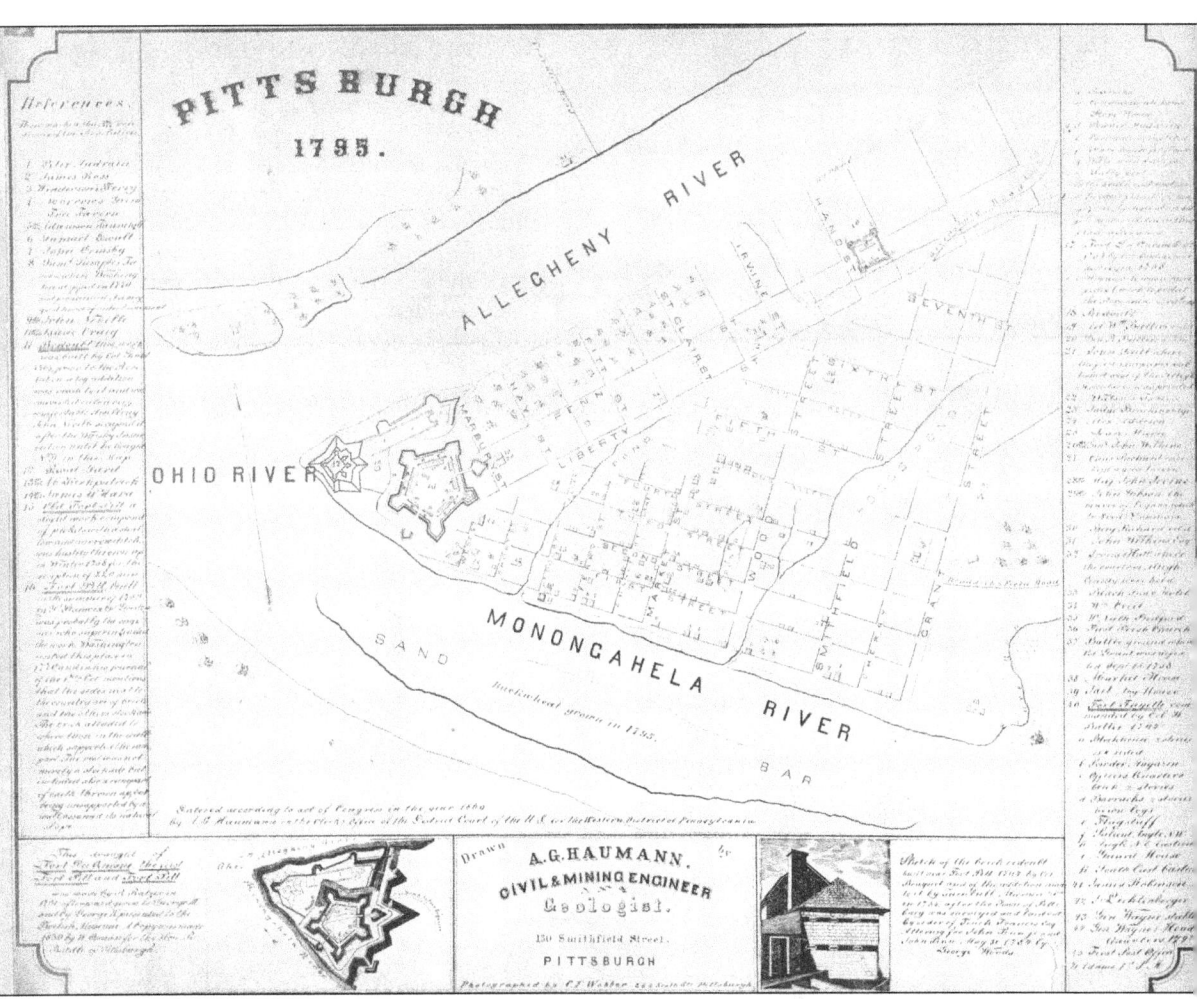

Among Pittsburgh's first settlers were the officers and soldiers of Fort Pitt, including Isaac Craig and Stephen Bayard, who in 1783 bought the first real estate sold by the Penn family at the forks. In 1764, the Penns had commissioned Fort Pitt's Col. John Campbell to lay out a street plan for the town, but it included only four blocks adjacent to the fort, along the Monongahela River. Twenty years later, Col. George Woods and his assistant, Thomas Vickroy, continued the plan to Grant Street and added two other streets, Penn and Liberty, parallel to the Allegheny, and a public square, a gift from the Penns, to hold a market house and courthouse. This map shows the location of Hogg's Pond and others that dotted the town for some years. In 1796, Pittsburgh had about 230 houses and 800 citizens. By 1802, eight barge builders, boatbuilders, and shipbuilders were producing an estimated $40,000 in flatboats, keelboats, canoes, and schooners, making boatbuilding the town's third-largest industry after iron and textiles. (Senator John Heinz History Center.)

THE COMMONWEALTH.

"Virtue, Liberty, and Independence."

PITTSBURGH, JANUARY 15, 1806.

Appointment by the Governor.

JOHN SMITH, Esq. (a federalist) register and recorder of Chester county, vice James Bones, Esq. (a republican) removed for opposing his excellency's re-election.

Duel.—The following particulars respecting the late duel are extracted from *The Pittsburgh Gazette* of yesterday.— From motives of delicacy, we decline, *at present*, making any remarks on the subject—reports, however, injurious to the character of the editor, and entirely destitute of foundation, having gone abroad, and been seized upon with avidity, by his political enemies, to blast his reputation— a vindication of his conduct will shortly be given to the public—until then he requests a suspension of public opinion.

Two years after Meriwether Lewis spent several weeks in Pittsburgh as his largest expedition boat was built, Tarleton Bates, his good friend from Virginia, became ensnared in a political argument that began with name-calling and ended in a duel. Bates, an editor of the *Tree of Liberty* newspaper, was shot and killed by merchant Thomas Stewart. Here the *Commonwealth* editor Ephraim Pentland, indirectly the cause of the duel, asks Pittsburghers not to rush to judgment about him.

BARNABAS M'SHANE,

Who has for some time past kept the Inn in Black Horse Alley, is now removed to that old and commodious Tavern,

The Harp and Crown,

In Third Street.

HE begs leave to solicit the favors of his friends and the public in general, and assures those gentlemen who formerly frequented that house and the Harp & Crown, that every accommodation, both for them-

The tavern was the center of community life in 1786 when this advertisement appeared in the *Gazette*. It served as theater, concert hall, town hall, ballroom, and even church. During the Whiskey Rebellion of 1794, Pittsburgh and its taverns were viewed by the rebels as supporters of the federal excise tax on whiskey. Lawyer Hugh Henry Brackenridge talked them out of burning down the town.

Two

A City's First Steps, Then Disaster
1816–1845

In the first half of the 19th century, Pittsburgh continued to play a role as a gateway to the west as the triangle filled in with houses and businesses, many of them outfitting or housing travelers by boat as they waited for the Monongahela and Ohio Rivers to rise to navigable levels. At the eastern edge of the triangle was Grant's Hill, which projected like a peninsula from the Bluff into the city. Named for British major James Grant, who was defeated there in a skirmish with the French in September 1858, it was by all accounts a cherished vantage point, promenade, and Fourth of July picnic spot, but one that would be gradually whittled away until it became merely an inconvenience dubbed "the Hump." In the early 1900s, that too would be removed, with heavy consequences for existing buildings such as H. H. Richardson's courthouse of 1888, now entered through its basement. In his *Letters from the West*, James Hall describes the city as seen from Grant's Hill in 1828:

> Grant's-hill, an abrupt eminence which projects into the rear of the city, affords one of the most delightful prospects with which I am acquainted; presenting a singular combination of the bustle of the town, with the solitude and sweetness of the country. How many hours have I spent here, in enjoyment of those exquisite sensations which are awakened by pleasing associations and picturesque scenes! The city lay beneath me, enveloped in smoke—the clang of hammers resounded from its numerous manufactories—the rattling of carriages and the hum of men were heard from its streets—churches, courts, hotels, and markets, and all the "pomp and circumstance" of busy life, were presented in one panoramic view. Behind me were all the silent soft attractions of rural sweetness—the ground rising gradually for a considerable distance, and exhibiting country seats, surrounded with cultivated fields, gardens, and orchards.

On March 18, 1816, Pittsburgh was elevated from borough to city. Maj. Ebenezer Denny, Revolutionary War soldier, merchant, and one-time partner of Gen. James O'Hara in house building, was appointed the first mayor by the select and common councils. Denny's 1781 war diary is an oft-cited account of the surrender of the British at Yorktown, Virginia. (Senator John Heinz History Center.)

Boys play in the water near keelboats tied up at the Monongahela wharf, about 1825. On Front Street was the first house (far left) of William Wilkins, whose later estate embraced much of Homewood and Wilkinsburg. Next to it was a woolen mill replaced in 1839 by the original Monongahela House hotel. Beyond the covered bridge at Smithfield Street were Irwin's tavern and Benjamin Page's glassworks. This image is from an oil by Leander McCandless. (Palmer's Pictorial Pittsburgh.)

Neville B. Craig, son of Isaac Craig and Amelia Neville, was born in 1787 in the blockhouse, to which his parents had attached an annex where they set up housekeeping. From 1829 to 1841, Craig was the influential publisher and editor of the *Pittsburgh Gazette*, founded in 1786 by John Scull, who brought a printing press over the mountains to establish the first newspaper west of the Alleghenies. Craig also authored the city's first published history (1851).

By 1837, travelers from Philadelphia could cross the state by taking the train to Harrisburg and then transferring to packet boats on the Pennsylvania Canal. Charles Dickens, traveling from Baltimore in 1842, took a packet boat from Harrisburg to Pittsburgh. In his *American Notes*, he writes that he found both the accommodations and the travelers primitive but in the end looked back on the adventure "with great pleasure."

Canal boats from the East arrived first at Allegheny City. Then they crossed the Allegheny River by aqueduct to a basin at the present site of the Pennsylvanian apartments (formerly Penn Station). For a time, it continued to the Monongahela River, partly through a short-lived tunnel under Grant's Hill.

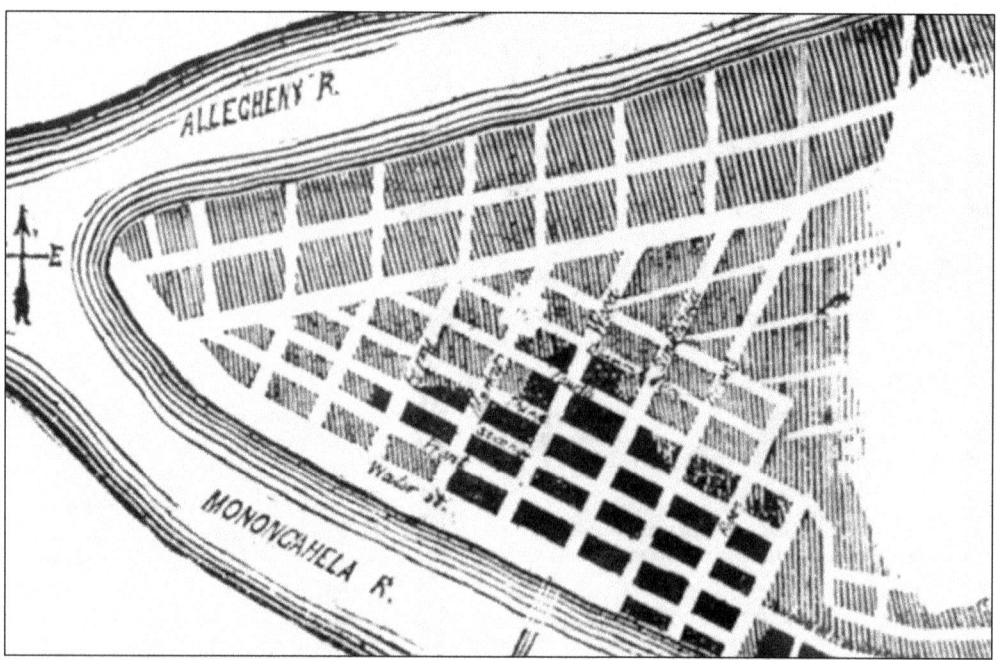
In 1845, a great fire consumed about 24 blocks in the heart of the city. It spread eastward beyond Grant Street into Pipetown (where William Price manufactured clay pipes, the site of the present PNC Firstside Center) before burning itself out on the side of Boyd's Hill (now the Bluff). (Pittsburgh Post-Gazette.)

![Great Conflagration at Pittsburgh]

From a washerwoman's open fire behind William Diehl's icehouse, at the corner of what is now Stanwix Street and Boulevard of the Allies, flames spread rapidly to engulf one-third of the city on April 10, 1845. Nearly 1,000 buildings and homes were destroyed, including Western University, Bank of Pittsburgh, Monongahela House, Globe Cotton Factory, and the customhouse. About 12,000 people were left homeless, but only two lives were lost. (Mrs. James A. Bell.)

This is Pittsburgh from Birmingham (South Side) two days after the fire, as captured then by Pittsburgh painter William Coventry Wall. "A doomed city," mourned newspapers everywhere, but merchants and residents quickly rebuilt. The sound of the hammer was everywhere, and out of the debris came stronger and handsomer structures of iron and brick, many in the Greek Revival style of the day. (Carnegie Museum of Art.)

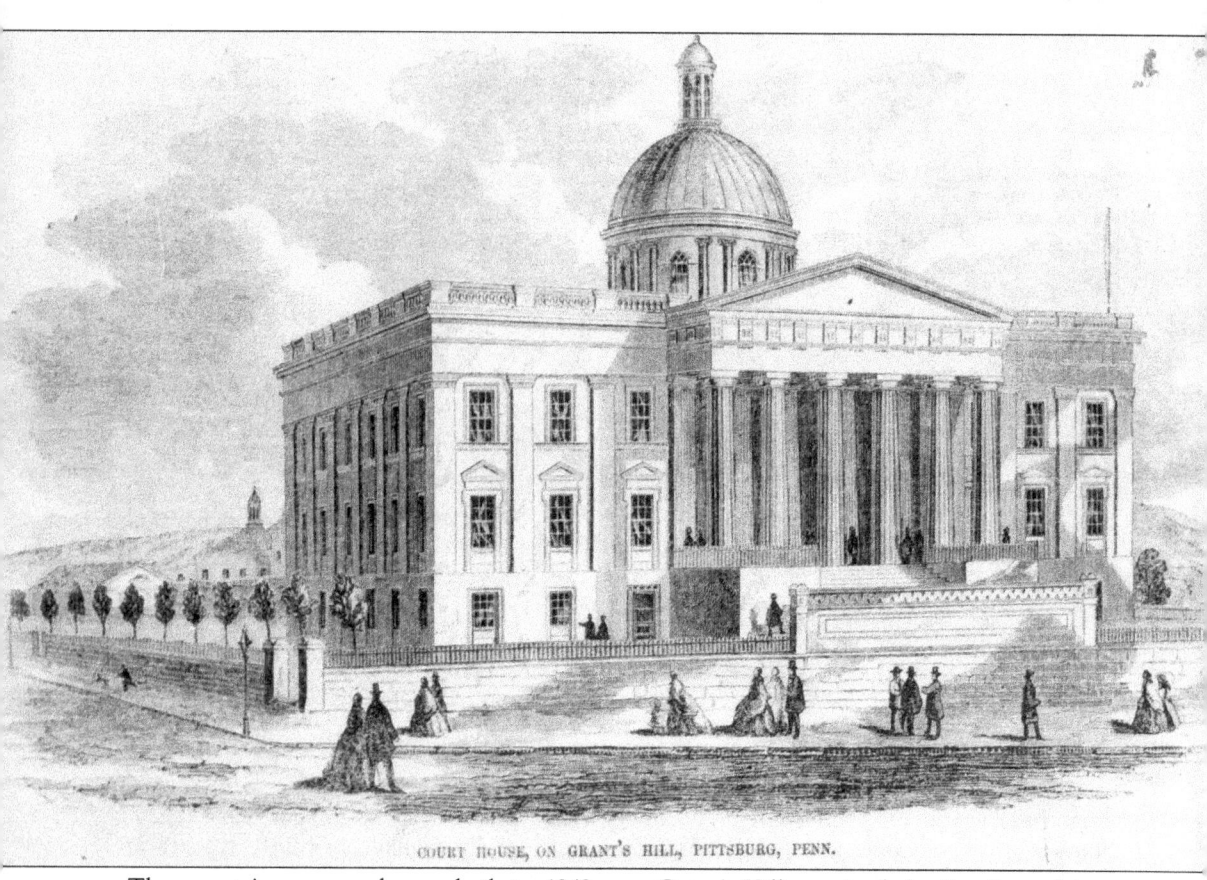

COURT HOUSE, ON GRANT'S HILL, PITTSBURG, PENN.

The county's new courthouse, built in 1842 atop Grant's Hill, survived the fire. Its architect was John Chislett, a native of Bath, England. Pittsburgh's first professional architect, he also designed the city's oldest office building—Burke's Building of 1836, at 211 Fourth Avenue—and the Romantic landscape of Allegheny Cemetery and its Butler Street gateway.

Three

PITTSBURGH REBUILDS AND EXPANDS
1846–1859

Pennsylvania was the first state to outlaw slavery, in 1780, but in the mid-19th century the debate about it was raging here as everywhere. As Pittsburgh recovered from the great fire, two newspapers published here—the *Mystery* and the *Pittsburgh Saturday Visiter*—argued for its abolition. Stephen Foster, meanwhile, thought to have been inspired by Charles Dickens's 1854 novel *Hard Times*, about life in smoky, industrial "Coketown," wrote the music and lyrics for a song that also has echoes of the Southern plantation, "Hard Times Come Again No More":

Let us pause in life's pleasures and count its many tears / While we all sup sorrow with the poor: / There's a song that will linger forever in our ears; / Oh! Hard Times, come again no more. / 'Tis the song, the sigh of the weary; / Hard Times, Hard Times, come again no more: / Many days you have lingered around my cabin door; / Oh! Hard Times, come again no more. / While we seek mirth and beauty and music light and gay / There are frail forms fainting at the door: / Though their voices are silent, their pleading looking will say / Oh! Hard Times come again no more. / There's a pale drooping maiden who toils her life away / With a worn heart whose better days are o'er: / Though her voice would be merry, 'tis sighing all the day / Oh! Hard Times, come again no more. / 'Tis a sign that is wafted across the troubled wave, / 'Tis a wail that is heard upon the shore, / 'Tis a dirge that is murmured around the lowly grave / Oh! Hard Times, come again no more.

One of several antislavery weeklies published in Pittsburgh was the *Mystery*, edited by Martin R. Delaney, a Harvard Medical School graduate. This issue of December 16, 1846, urged Pres. James Polk to accept African American soldiers for the Mexican War. A major with the 104th Regiment at Charleston, South Carolina, Delaney was the first African American field officer to serve in the Civil War. (Carnegie Library of Pittsburgh.)

On the day that Thomas Jefferson and John Adams died, July 4, 1826, Stephen Collins Foster, America's first professional songwriter, was born in a cottage in Lawrenceville. He wrote 189 songs in his short, troubled life, many of them melodic, sentimental ballads. Inspiration also came from slave songs, blackface minstrel songs, and the African American dialect he heard while working on the Cincinnati wharf as a clerk for his brother's steamboat company. (Stephen Foster Memorial Museum.)

The first Pittsburgh woman to dent the man's world was abolitionist Jane Grey Swisshelm, shown with her daughter. From 1848 to 1854, she published the *Pittsburgh Saturday Visiter*, mainly to further her crusades against slavery and for women's rights. Through her efforts, Pennsylvania passed a law allowing married women to own property. (Senator John Heinz History Center.)

23

German-born John Roebling developed the first wire rope in 1841 on his farm in Saxonburg and adapted it to the canal aqueduct across the Allegheny River. In 1845–1847, he used wire rope in the design of the world's first cable suspension bridge across the Monongahela River at Smithfield Street, which replaced a covered bridge lost in the great fire. His work on this and the second Sixth Street Bridge of 1859 established him as America's most prominent bridge engineer two decades before he designed the Brooklyn Bridge. (J&L Steel Corporation, Roebling Corporation.)

Gazette editor David N. White published the first call for formation of a Pennsylvania Republican Party in 1855. He also was a founder of the national party, which completed organization in Pittsburgh at its first national convention in February 1856. The sessions were held in Lafayette Hall on Fourth Street near Wood Street. Lawrence Brainard of Vermont, in opening the convention, said, the meeting "is simply to organize the Republican party and put forth the principles, which are, as I understand them, the same as those by which our independence was achieved, on which our Constitution is established, and if we do our part with justice, wisdom and moderation, the country and the Union will be perpetuated." Built around 1850, Lafayette Hall was razed in 1895.

By 1860, rails were being rolled in large quantities to meet the demands of rapidly expanding railroads, and Pittsburgh's iron industry boomed. Major furnaces and mills included those of the Kloman Brothers; Jones, Lauth and Company; and Laughlin and Company. (J&L Steel Corporation.)

Acclaimed as one of the finest church buildings in the United States, St. Paul Cathedral, consecrated in 1855, was at the corner of Grant Street and Fifth Avenue, site of the present Two Mellon Center (Union Arcade). In the 1870s, Allegheny City native Mary Cassatt painted a mural in Italy for the cathedral; it is thought to have been destroyed in a fire that consumed a cathedral chapel in 1877.

On December 10, 1852, a crowd gathered in East Liberty to welcome the first through-train from the East, which had scaled the mountains via inclined planes. In 1854, after a tunnel had been built, the *Gazette* proclaimed, "Fifteen hours from Pittsburgh to Philadelphia ought to satisfy the fastest of this fast generation." This was one of the earliest outdoor crowd photographs made here. (Pennsylvania Railroad.)

A $500 draft was found by a messenger for the O'Reilly Telegraph Company and, said the *Gazette* on November 2, 1849, "like an honest little fellow," he returned it. A few years later the messenger, Andrew Carnegie, shown here at 16 with his younger brother Thomas, was an official of the Pennsylvania Railroad. (*Autobiography of Andrew Carnegie*, Houghton Mifflin Company, 1920.)

From 1803 on, touring theatrical companies staged plays in Pittsburgh, choosing secondary roles from the amateur acting societies. The Pittsburgh Theater, better known as the Old Drury, was on Fifth Avenue near Wood Street. "We all fell under the fascination of the footlights, and every opportunity to attend the theater was eagerly embraced," Carnegie recalled of his visits there as a telegraph messenger boy admitted for free at age 15.

Pittsburgh's first fire brigade, the Eagle Volunteer Fire Company, was organized in 1794, and by 1815, it was competing with the Vigilant and Neptune companies for subscribers. In 1859, Eagle acquired this steam engine, manufactured by the Duquesne Way plant of James Rees, steamboat and engine builder. The man in the left inset was the son of William Peter Eichbaum, the German-born developer of James O'Hara's glassworks, which produced bottles for his brewery. When Eichbaum's home was destroyed in the great fire of 1845, he moved east of the city and built an elegant Greek Revival home above Fifth Avenue, on the site of the University of Pittsburgh Medical Center Montefiore, from the brick of a deserted barn. Eichbaum ("oak tree" in German) is said to have called his nine-acre estate Oakland for its native trees. Eichbaum purchased his land from James Chadwick, who started his 1,000-acre Oakland Farm in 1806. From one or both of these sources, the name was adopted for the neighborhood. (Senator John Heinz History Center.)

On the occasion of the city's 100th birthday, many Pittsburghers stopped at Hunt and Miner's bookstore on Fifth Street (now Fifth Avenue) to buy a copy of the centennial celebration keepsake. The author/editor, Joseph M. Kinkead, hoped in print that purchasers would "lay away a copy of this, neatly folded, in the family Bible" or elsewhere. (Edwin P. Brown.)

Four

THE CIVIL WAR AND THE IRON CITY
1860–1879

Pittsburgh's industrial might grew during the Civil War, as businesses and residents mobilized to support the Union. Ten years after the war, a new kind of metal was born, one that would transform the Iron City into the Steel City. In 1868, writing in the *Atlantic Monthly*, James Parton coined the phrase that would define the city for the next 120 years:

> Smoke, smoke, everywhere smoke! Smoke with the noise of the steam hammer, and the spouting flame of tall chimneys / On the evening of this dark day we were conducted to the edge of the abyss, and looked over the iron railing upon the most striking spectacle we ever beheld. The entire space lying between the hills was filled with the blackest smoke, from out of which the hidden chimneys sent forth tongues of flame, while from the depths of the abyss came up the noise of hundreds of steam hammers / soon the wind would force the smoky curtains aside and the whole black expanse would be dimly lighted with dull wreaths of fire / if any one would enjoy a spectacle as striking as Niagara, he may do so by simply walking up a long hill to Cliff Street in Pittsburgh and looking over into—hell with the lid taken off.

The Rodman Gun was one of many produced during the Civil War by the C. Knapp Foundry. Named for Lt. Thomas J. Rodman, commander of the Allegheny Arsenal, it was the largest in the world. The man at right in this photograph was foundry superintendent Joseph Kaye. Pittsburgh factories supplied the Union with warships, armor plate, shot, shells, saddles, harnesses, wagons, gun carriages, caissons, clothing, and a variety of other war materials.

The Pittsburgh Sanitary Commission was organized early in the war to send medical aid to the front lines. On one such expedition, physician Felix R. Brunot was captured with a field hospital and held a short time in Libby Prison. Under Brunot's direction, the Sanitary Fair was staged on the Allegheny Commons in June 1864; it raised $322,217. Its bazaar, shown here, had about 40 booths and a platform where musicians offered such tunes as "When this Civil War Is Over."

One of Pittsburgh's outstanding military figures was Maj. Gen. James Scott Negley, the hatless officer shown with his men on Lookout Mountain during a lull in the Battle of Chattanooga. A veteran of the Mexican War and later commander of the state militia, he saw action through the Shenandoah and Tennessee campaigns and won a promotion for heroic service at Murfreesboro. After a retreat at Chickamauga, he was relieved of his command by Gen. William S. Rosencrans, who later had his own command lifted. Negley demanded a court of inquiry and was cleared of an unfounded charge of cowardice. He then resigned, returned to Pittsburgh, served in Congress four times and retired to New York City, where he became president of the Mexican Trust Company bank.

Nine deposits were made on a hot day in July 1855, when the Pittsburgh Dollar Savings Institution opened its doors. Its Fourth Avenue building, designed by Philadelphia architect Isaac Hobbs and completed in 1871, still stands. Behind its red sandstone facade is the oldest intact interior space in downtown Pittsburgh, designed in the classical style with pilasters lining the walls and a large medallion in the ceiling.

Born in Ireland, Thomas Mellon grew up on a Westmoreland County farm, attended Western University, hung out a law shingle in 1839, married Sarah Jane Negley in 1843, and fathered eight children. After 10 years as judge of common pleas court, he opened T. Mellon and Sons Bank on Smithfield Street, which backed much of Pittsburgh's industrial growth. This oil portrait was painted by Theobald Chartran, probably about 1880.

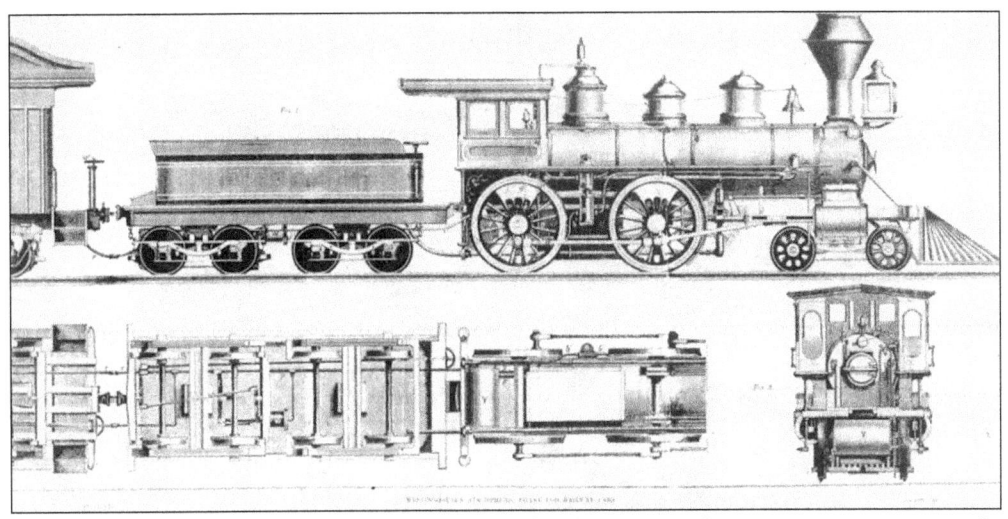

George Westinghouse was 19 when he obtained his first patent, for a rotary steam engine. In 1869, at 22, he introduced the air brake, the first effective means for stopping heavy trains, and started manufacturing it in a plant at Twenty-ninth Street and Liberty Avenue. So began a remarkable career that included such advancements as alternating current, natural gas supply, the safety signal, and the electric locomotive. (*American Mechanical Dictionary*, 1877.)

George Anschutz built the first iron furnace here in 1792, Joseph McClurg the first foundry in 1803. In Kentucky, another Pittsburgher, William Kelly, experimented with a new kind of metal in 1847, and in England, Henry Bessemer developed steelmaking out of Kelly's process. In 1875, on Braddock's Field, Andrew Carnegie opened the first plant to produce Bessemer steel on a mass scale. Its first order was 2,000 steel rails for the mill's namesake, Pennsylvania Railroad president J. Edgar Thomson.

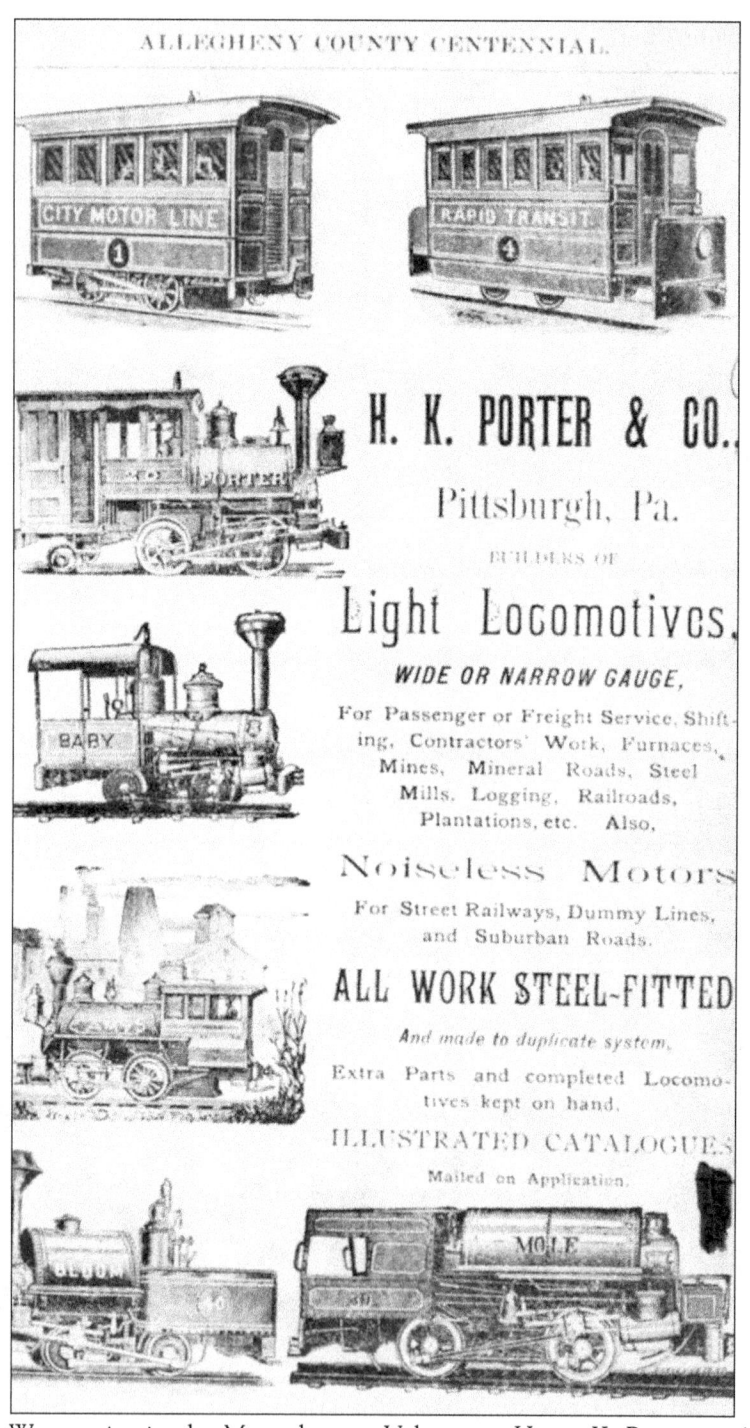

After Civil War service in the Massachusetts Volunteers, Henry K. Porter, in 1866, began producing light switching locomotives in a Lawrenceville plant under the name Smith and Porter. The firm continued making locomotives, as many as 600 a year, until 1939, when it entered into widely diversified fields. This 1888 advertisement is from *Allegheny County, Its Early History and Subsequent Developments*.

"Riot Law Triumphant—the Reign of Anarchy in the Smoky City," the *Gazette* headline read. On July 19, 1877, Pennsylvania Railroad workers joined their brethren in other cities and struck to protest wage cuts and layoffs. When police and local militia sided with the strikers, troops were called from Philadelphia. On July 21, after strikers and their supporters directed a barrage of stones and a revolver shot at the troops, they fired into the crowd, killing 20 men, women, and children and wounding 29. Millworkers, miners, and other workers soon joined the riot, and troops took cover in a roundhouse. Strikers set fires that destroyed dozens of railroad cars and buildings, including the Union Depot and Hotel, built in 1854 at Grant Street and Liberty Avenue. The scene was captured by Fred B. Schell for *Harper's Weekly*. Another *Harper's* artist, J. W. Alexander, was pelted with eggs as he sketched on a nearby rooftop. Troops shot their way out of the roundhouse and left the city. The tumult left 61 people dead and 150 injured and caused $7 million in property damage.

First to mass-produce coke in beehive ovens, a major factor in the opening of the steel industry, was Henry Clay Frick. At 14, in 1863, he was earning $3.50 a week as an errand boy for a store in Mount Pleasant. In five years, he was buying coal lands, determined to make coke. This continued through the panic of 1873, when coke dropped to 90¢ a ton, forcing out many small companies. By the late 1880s, the "Coke King" had 10,000 ovens with 11,000 employees in the Connellsville area. This was an exhibit at the 1893 Chicago world's fair.

| B. F. JONES | SAMUEL KIER | BERNARD LAUTH |
| JAMES LAUGHLIN | THOMAS M. JONES | WILLIAM L. JONES |

In 1853, Benjamin F. Jones, Bernard (and John) Lauth, and Samuel M. Kier joined in iron making on the south bank of the Monongahela River. Kier, under whom Jones had worked on the *Mechanics Line* canal boat, left the firm a short time later to refine oil. Across the river, James Laughlin, a banker, built blast furnaces in 1859 and later merged with the Jones brothers. When the firm was reorganized as the J&L Steel Corporation in 1923, William Larimer Jones, son of Thomas M. Jones, was elected president.

Crude oil from the Titusville area, where Col. Edwin L. Drake had brought in the first well in 1859, was transported down the Allegheny River by flatboat. Oil traders like these, around 1869, met the boats and transacted business on the Duquesne Way wharf. Out of such operations came the Pittsburgh Petroleum Exchange, with business volume averaging four million barrels per day by 1885.

Pittsburgh was not all work. In the 1870s, one might enjoy Carncross and Dixey's Minstrels at Library Hall, Madame Rentz's Female Minstrels at the Academy of Music, or Sarah Bernhardt and Helena Modjeska at the opera house. Here is an 1879 playbill.

Here is an idealized view of the corner of Fifth Avenue and Craig Street, Oakland, in the 1870s as gingerbread trimmings came into vogue with the lathe and jigsaw. This Italianate house, designed by Isaac Hobbs for insurance agent A. A. Carrier, later was the music-filled home of window-glass manufacturer Robert C. Schmertz, grandfather and namesake of the architect who wrote and sang such Pittsburgh folk songs as "Monongahela Sal." The house was razed in 1956 to build the University Square apartments.

Following the war, Pittsburgh's glass industry continued to grow, at one time comprising 62 separate factories. A number were in Birmingham (South Side), such as this one, and nearby boroughs.

On the horsecar's inaugural run on August 6, 1859, the *Gazette* was pleased to observe interior straps, which a passenger could grasp and "ride as pleasantly as though he were sitting." Here is a car on upper Fifth Avenue in 1879. The first cable car, in 1889, cut the horse's traveling time, downtown to East End, from as many as 100 minutes to 30. But the cables could not switch from main to branch lines and soon were supplanted by electric trolleys.

Here is Pittsburgh in 1874 from Allegheny City's Hogback Hill (later Monument Hill). This view includes a smoke-billowing steamer at the Duquesne Way wharf and Roebling's Sixth Street Bridge. By 1880, Allegheny's population was 78,682 and Pittsburgh's 156,381, the latter having doubled in that decade mainly as a result of annexations. The biggest acquisition, Allegheny City itself, was still to come, in 1907. (*Picturesque America*, Vol. II, 1874.)

Five

THE GILDED AGE OF INDUSTRY
1880–1899

Against the backdrop of the Gilded Age stands the lockout and strike at Homestead in 1892. In hilly Pittsburgh, the contrasts between the haves and have-nots was evident to all: the city was filling up, with millworkers' frame houses along narrow, terraced, switchback streets, and with elegant mansions on broad, tree-lined avenues for mill executives and owners. With most workers pulling 12-hour shifts six or seven days a week, Andrew Carnegie began to return some of his great wealth to the community in public libraries and museums. He had advice—certainly it had worked for him—for those who questioned his unwavering, intensive focus on a single industry: "Concentrate; put all your eggs in one basket, and watch that basket."

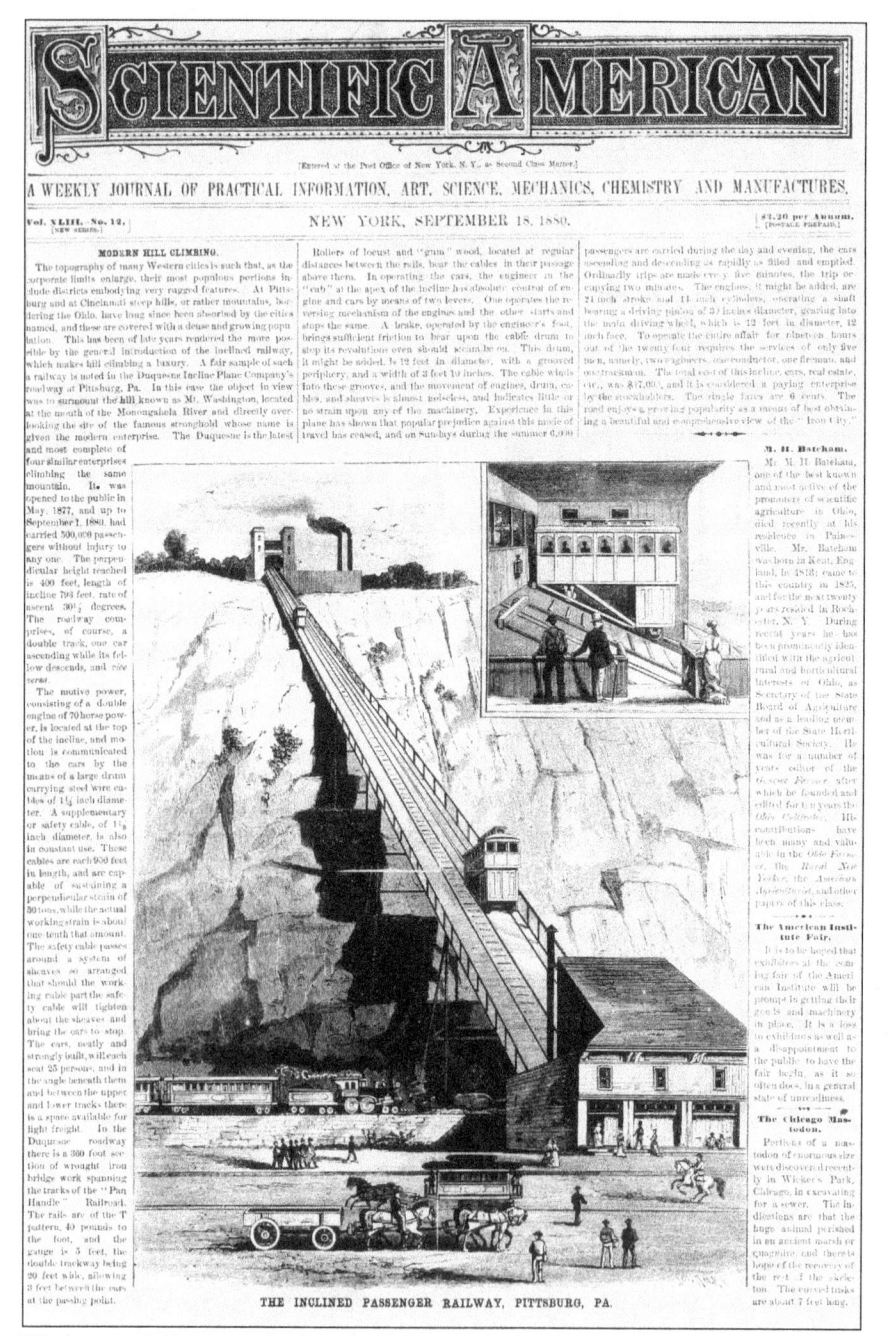

Mount Washington's Duquesne Incline, built in 1877 for $47,000, had attracted 500,000 passengers "without injury to any one" by 1880, when this illustration appeared in *Scientific American*. "Experience in this plane has shown that popular prejudice against this mode of travel has ceased, and on Sundays during the summer 6,000 passengers are carried during the day and evening; the cars ascending and descending as rapidly as filled and emptied," it wrote. "The road enjoys a growing popularity as a means of best obtaining a beautiful and comprehensive view of the 'Iron City.'" The Monongahela, the city's first incline, began in 1870. Both survive as working reminders of the 17 inclines that once connected Pittsburgh's hills and valleys.

The Smithfield Street Bridge, designed by Gustav Lindenthal and opened in 1883 as successor to Roebling's span, separated carriage and wagon traffic from horse-drawn trolleys. The portals, with their mansard roofs, remained until the bridge was modernized in 1915. A full rehabilitation was completed in the mid-1990s, including restoration of the original paint scheme and six copper finials on the portals.

"If they honor me for the pigmy things I have done, what will they say when they see Pittsburgh finished?" So said architect Henry Hobson Richardson about his Allegheny County Courthouse and Jail, which instantly became one of America's most admired and imitated architectural works. Built to replace John Chislett's courthouse, which had been destroyed by fire in 1882, it is shown here in its original form in 1889, a year after completion.

"Tennis girls" are pictured around 1886 in front of Berry Hall at Pittsburgh Female College, chartered in 1868 to give young women opportunities for higher education denied them by all-male Western University. The name was changed in 1890 to Pennsylvania College for Women and changed again in 1955 to Chatham College, honoring William Pitt, first earl of Chatham. In 2007, it became Chatham University.

The Duquesne Club's famed "Number Six" luncheon group is shown in 1892, with members composing the backbone of Pittsburgh industry and business. Pictured are, from left to right, (first row) S. Schoyer Jr., Campbell B. Herron, B. F. Jones Sr., John W. Chalfant, and M. K. Moorhead; (second row) John H. Ricketson, A. E. W. Painter, Charles L. Fitzhugh, George Shiras Jr. (named the same year to the U.S. Supreme Court), Albert H. Childs, Frank H. Phipps, and C. N. Spang.

One of the bloodiest strikes in American labor history began as a lockout by Henry Clay Frick at Carnegie Steel's Homestead Works. It ended with at least 14 dead—11 steelworkers and 3 Pinkerton guards. Frick had sealed off the mill—Fort Frick, the workers called it—and hired about 300 Pinkertons to protect it. In the early morning of July 6, 1892, as the guards approached the mill on river barges under cover of darkness, they were met by steelworkers and their families. No one knows who fired the first shot, but for several hours, the Battle of Homestead raged. With their barges burning, the Pinkertons surrendered and were forced to walk a gauntlet through strikers. But the company soon hired replacement workers, eventually breaking the Amalgamated Association of Iron and Steelworkers and setting back the cause of labor 30 years. Homestead's Bost Building, headquarters of the Amalgamated Association in 1892, now houses the Rivers of Steel Visitors Center and its exhibits, including a 23-foot-long model of the Homestead Works that once stood in the general office building of the mill.

Rising some 250 feet (about 25 stories) above the Midway Plaissance of the 1893 World's Columbian Exposition in Chicago was a "big wheel from Pittsburgh." Designed and erected by engineer George W. G. Ferris, it proved to be the fair's biggest attraction. In 19 weeks, 1,453,611 customers paid $726,805 to ride in its 36 glass-enclosed coaches. Ferris was living in a modest brick house at 204 (now 1318) Arch Street in Allegheny City when he designed the wheel.

Cycling parties peddling out Fifth Avenue always stopped at Howe Spring, at Highland Avenue, for a cool drink of pure springwater. The fountain there was erected in memory of industrialist Thomas M. and Mary Ann Palmer Howe, whose home, Greystone, was built on the hill above before the Civil War. The cycling boom gave rise to many inns such as Wheelman's Retreat and Cycler's Rest.

The 1893 second-place Pirates were one of baseball's strongest-hitting clubs. Jake Stenzel (No. 17 above) batted .409; Elmer Smith (2), .366; and George Van Haltren (7), .350. The catcher was Connie Mack (9), the club's manager for three seasons after succeeding Al Buckenberger (14) in 1894. Louis Bierbauer (11) was the disputed player over whom the Pirates got their name after signing a loose infielder claimed by the American Association.

Steamboats and coal barges often crowded the Monongahela River in 1896, when this picture was made. Meeting at the Point were the covered Union Bridge (left) and the suspension Point Bridge. Near the bridge junction, on the Allegheny bank, were buildings of the Pittsburgh Exposition, which presented such novelties as a Ferris wheel, merry-go-round, gravity railroad, cinematograph, and Colonel Baker's popcorn stand. The last exposition was in 1918.

Andrew Carnegie founded the Carnegie International in 1896 "for the masses of the people primarily, not for the educated few." It would bring the art world to Pittsburgh and build a collection of contemporary art through purchase of the "Old Masters of tomorrow." Today it is the oldest exhibition of international contemporary art in North America, second oldest in the world.

Here is Schenley Farms in the spring of 1899, from Centre Avenue Hill, site of the University of Pittsburgh's upper campus after 1908. The Schenley Hotel, just opened the previous fall, is seen across the future site of Soldiers and Sailors Memorial Hall. To the left is the new Carnegie Institute; to the right is St. Pierre Ravine, later filled in to create Schenley Plaza. In the background are Schenley Park and the peaceful countryside of Squirrel Hill.

Six

A New Century, a World War
1900–1919

As the steel industry continued to dominate Pittsburgh's landscape and climate, the lives of workers and their families drew national attention with the publication of A *Pittsburgh Survey*, the first and most complete analysis of urban conditions in the United States. Funded by the Russell Sage Foundation, nearly 70 researchers, along with photographer Lewis Hine and artist Joseph Stella, began in 1907 to produce a landmark work in six volumes, including Margaret Byington's *Homestead: The Households of a Mill Town*. Here she describes typical courtyard housing:

> From the cinder path beside one of the railroads that crosses the level part of Homestead, you enter an alley, bordered on one side by stables and on the other by a row of shabby two-story frame houses. The doors of the houses are closed, but dishpans and old clothes decorating their exterior mark them as inhabited. Turning from the alley through a narrow passageway you find yourself in a small court, on three sides of which are smoke-grimed houses, and on the fourth, low stables. The open space teems with life and movement. Children, dogs and hens make it lively under foot; overhead long lines of flapping clothes must be dodged. A group of women stand gossiping in one corner awaiting their turn at the pump, which is one of the two sources of water supply for the 20 families who live here. Another woman dumps the contents of her washtubs upon the paved ground, and the greasy, soapy water runs into an open drain a few feet from the pump. In the center a circular wooden building with ten compartments opening into one vault, flushed only by this waste water, constitutes the toilet accommodations for over one hundred people. Twenty-seven children find in this crowded brick-paved space their only playground; for the 63 rooms in the houses above the court shelter a group of 20 families, Polish, Slavic and Hungarian, Jewish and Negro. The men are unskilled workers in the mills.

Straw hats, an open trolley car, and a newsboy share the scene with the newly built 24-story Farmers Bank Building (left, at Wood Street), then tallest in the city. Frank Leslie's Weekly, in the March 19, 1903, issue devoted to Pittsburgh, featured the Farmers Bank and Frick buildings. Of the latter, opened in 1902, it wrote, "Who would even think to look for the finest office building in the world in Pittsburg, Penn.?" By 1905, downtown Pittsburgh had a dozen structures of skyscraper height. "Let them multiply," cheered the *Pittsburgh Bulletin*. "There is no sky in the world which needs scraping more than that which arches over the Iron City." Pittsburgh lost its *h* in 1890 when the U.S. Board on Geographic Names, for consistency's sake, went with the majority spelling for towns ending in *burg* or *burgh*. After much lobbying, Pittsburgh had the historic spelling restored in 1911.

Luna Park opened on May 25, 1905, on the old Aspinwall estate, with its main entrance at the present corner of Craig Street and Baum Boulevard. It attracted crowds of up to 35,000 people nightly who came for the aerial acts, band concerts, and a shoot-the-chutes ride into a pool of water. But after a menagerie lion escaped and killed a woman in 1907, its popularity waned. After a fire at the park two years later, it was not rebuilt.

After the 1923 opening of King Tutankhamen's tomb, Kennywood Park changed the theme of its Bug House dark ride to Tut's Tomb the following year. In 1995, the park took inspiration for its Lost Kennywood addition from Luna Park's shoot-the-chutes and its surrounding buildings.

53

On January 9, 1901, on the eve of formation of the United States Steel Corporation, 89 executives of Carnegie companies gathered for dinner in the Schenley Hotel ballroom. One of them was Charles Schwab who, fearing the Carnegie-Rockefeller steel war would have disastrous results, pleaded for industrial peace and growth through consolidation. Banker J. Pierpoint Morgan obliged, buying out Carnegie and eight other steel firms. (R. W. Johnston.)

At a Homestead boardinghouse about 1909, Slavic mill workers were photographed by Lewis Hine. The picture appeared among many of his images in the *Pittsburgh Survey*, published in 1910 by the Russell Sage Foundation. This six-volume work, the most comprehensive sociological study made in this country to that time, helped bring about social reforms both here and in other large cities.

Andrew Carnegie, right, built his one-man rule on a competitive system that rewarded the shrewdest and strongest with partnership. Henry Clay Frick, who ran Carnegie's steel mills, believed in corporate interdependence and rule by directors. This clash of philosophies led to a long feud.

Both Carnegie and Frick left cultural legacies in Pittsburgh, Carnegie with his museums, libraries, and university, and Frick with the Frick Art and Historical Center—the house, art, and carriage museums established by his daughter, Helen Clay Frick. In New York, Carnegie's mansion is now the Cooper Hewitt National Design Museum and Frick's home is the Frick Collection.

The bustling produce belt in the 600 block of Liberty Avenue is pictured about 1906 looking west toward the Jenkins and Empire buildings in the background. The street shows three sets of streetcar tracks and a rather jumbled "English pattern" of left-side traffic movement.

Here is the Smithfield Street business block, between Virgin Alley (later Oliver Avenue) and Sixth Avenue, just before it was cleared in 1908–1909 for erection of the 25-story Oliver Building. The fourth building from the right, housing the William E. Stieren Company, was the original home of Mellon Bank at 145 (later 541) Smithfield in 1869. Stieren, an optician, established his business in 1863 as a manufacturer of and dealer in scientific instruments.

George W. Guthrie was elected mayor in 1906 on a Democratic anticorruption platform and served four years. In 1913, Pres. Woodrow Wilson appointed Guthrie ambassador to Japan, where he died four years later. He is shown in 1908 reviewing the police force, a Thanksgiving Day ritual for many years. With him is safety director Edward Lang. Guthrie coauthored the Pittsburgh–Allegheny City merger bill. (Carnegie Library of Pittsburgh, Bingaman Collection.)

In 1909, the Pirates, under Fred Clarke, won 110 league games and the World Series. One reason was a bowlegged infielder from Carnegie: John Peter Wagner, league batting champ in 8 of 12 seasons from 1900 through 1911. Honus (short for Johannes, his first name in German) Wagner (center) and another all-time great, Ty Cobb (right) of the Detroit Tigers, discuss bats during the 1909 series at the new Forbes Field. (Carnegie Library of Pittsburgh, Bingaman Collection.)

On a 1909 visit to dedicate Memorial Fountain in Arsenal Park, Pres. William H. Taft saw the Pirates lose to Chicago at Exposition Park. As he enjoyed Honus Wagner's double, his picture was taken by Frank Bingaman, and the next day it appeared in the *Gazette-Times' Illustrated Sunday Magazine*. A year later, when Taft was here for Carnegie Institute's Founder's Day and another ball game, he was greeted by a blown-up version of the same photograph on a billboard near the new Forbes Field. (Carnegie Library of Pittsburgh.)

In 1910, Cumberland W. Posey, son of one of the founders of the *Pittsburgh Courier*, organized a group of Homestead steelworkers into what was to be one of baseball's greatest clubs and gate attractions. In later years, the Homestead Grays won eight out of nine National Negro League titles. Among its stars was the mighty home-run hitter Josh Gibson. Posey is shown (third from left, second row) with his 1913 team.

Box seats were full at the Alvin Theater on Sixth Street for a benefit showing of Gilbert and Sullivan's comic opera *The Pirates of Penzance* in June 1908. When the Alvin opened in 1891, the *Gazette* wrote that it was the finest theater in the state and had few equals in the country.

For many years the Union News Stand at the Carnegie Depot served railroad travelers and commuters with newspapers, magazines, tobacco, candy, and parcel-checking service. It is shown around 1911, when it was operated by Leonard McMillen; the man and two boys are unidentified.

Homeward-bound commuters are pictured at Pennsylvania Station during the 1907 flood. Railroads were a major mode of transit for some 50 years. In 1910, East Liberty alone was served by 104 trains a day, and in peak hours, railroads scheduled 12,323 seats out of downtown, compared with 23,942 on street railway lines. In 1922, the peak year, 368 daily commuter trains operated in the Pittsburgh district. The automobile caused a decline to 67 by 1947.

The triangular Wabash Terminal, at Ferry Street (now Stanwix) and Liberty Avenue, was a busy travel center from 1904 to 1913, the years of rise and fall of George Jay Gould's railroad empire. The $800,000 Beaux-Arts palace was an office building until 1953, when it was razed for development of Gateway Center. This became the site in 1958 of the seventh skyscraper to go up in the 25-acre commercial center.

Two eras overlap outside the Baltimore and Ohio Railroad station at Smithfield Street and Water Street (now Fort Pitt Boulevard). Some of the city's earliest taxicabs and two of the last of the horse-drawn hansom cabs compete for train arrivals in 1911. Designed by Philadelphia architect Frank Furness, the station occupied the Monongahela Wharf site from 1877 until 1956, when it was razed for construction of the Penn-Lincoln Parkway. (Baltimore and Ohio Railroad.)

From a three-quarter-acre horseradish patch he planted in 1869 in Sharpsburg, Henry J. Heinz built a multimillion-dollar food business. At his death in 1919, he was succeeded by his sons: Howard, as president, and Clifford, as vice president. He is seen about 1904 with Clifford at Greenlawn, the Heinz estate at 7009 Penn Avenue in Point Breeze.

Gulf Oil opened the world's first drive-in service station on December 1, 1913, on Baum Boulevard at the corner of South St. Clair Street, East End. Previously, gas pumps were located at curbs and automobiles parked on city streets to be serviced. Gulf Oil, founded in 1901, pioneered in many phases of motoring. (Gulf Oil Corporation.)

Banker Richard Beatty Mellon is flanked by his daughter, Sarah, and son Richard in this 1918 photograph taken at the Carrick home of mining supply company president and conservationist John M. Phillips, who founded the Pennsylvania Game Commission and cofounded the Boy Scouts of America. Four of the six children are those of Phillips and his wife, Harriet Duff, a noted crusader for social and humanitarian causes. (Mrs. Joseph Shuman.)

In the world of science, Dr. John A. Brashear was known and honored for his precision instruments and lenses, which made possible many of the most important astronomical discoveries of this century. In his own South Side Slopes neighborhood, he was to all "Uncle John," a gentle, understanding man who loved children and was loved in return. (Brashear Association.)

Here is laundry day in the Hill District, where once stood the country homes of the wealthy. Jewish, Irish, and Italian immigrants settled in tenements in the Hill District, which later also attracted African Americans from the South. This was Bustrick Way in 1919, near Washington Place's pushcarts and Logan Street's kosher shops, all now extinct. (William Rimmel.)

Steel mills blanketed the Strip District in 1919, when the newly formed Urban League of Pittsburgh organized the Lawrenceville Community Uplift Club, a group of 35 steelworkers' wives who cared for the sick and needy and sponsored social events. The women may have been part of the wave of migration of Southern black men and their families to Pittsburgh for steel jobs in the early decades of the 20th century.

To gain support for women's right to vote, Jennie Bradley Roessing in 1915 drove a "Liberty Bell" truck over the rural roads of Pennsylvania, traveling to and speaking in all 67 counties. The truck carried a Women's Liberty Bell, a life-size replica of Philadelphia's. A nationally known suffragist, Roessing and her husband, Frank, lived at 5506 Harriet Street in the East End in 1920, the year women voted here for the first time.

Here are Gay Nineties brides, all out of the Social Register and still fitting into their wedding dresses, in a 1914 reunion picture; with them are some of their grooms. (R. W. Johnston.)

In the fall of 1917, sweethearts and families assemble on the Duquesne Way wharf to bid sad adieu to Pittsburgh's first contingent of draftees. This scene was just below the old Sixth Street Bridge and embraces the elevated railroad trestle, which, for a half century, connected the Pennsylvania Railroad station at Eleventh Street with the freight yards at the Point. (William Rimmel.)

In 1916, Troop H, 1st Pennsylvania Calvary, departed for duty on the Mexican border; it was formed in 1911 by Col. Charles C. "Buck" McGovern. At her Penn Avenue home in Point Breeze, actress Lillian Russell Moore, wife of *Pittsburgh Leader* publisher Alexander Moore, hands a soldier's kit to Charles McGovern Jr., as his father (standing) looks on. (Charles C. McGovern.)

With 1,000 soldiers standing at attention in front of the College of Fine Arts on the Carnegie Tech campus, the Langley Aeronautical Laboratory was dedicated on April 2, 1918. The speaker, Dr. John A. Brashear, asked that it be named in memory of his good friend and fellow scientist Samuel P. Langley. In this structure, built in 29 days, servicemen were trained for wartime duty as airplane mechanics and riggers. (Carnegie Mellon University.)

In June 1919, soldiers of the 80th Infantry Division parade on Penn Avenue in East Liberty after a year in France. Many Pittsburghers also saw action with the 28th Division. The Enright Theater, on Penn, was named for Thomas F. Enright of the North Side, the first American soldier killed in the war. (80th Infantry Division Association.)

Seven

A Skyscraper University Grows in Oakland
1920–1939

The movement east to Oakland began in earnest after the great fire of 1845 and intensified with the development of Schenley Farms, the Carnegie museums and library complex, Carnegie Technical Schools (now Carnegie Mellon University), and the relocation of the University of Pittsburgh from the North Side's Observatory Hill to the Schenley Farms hillside in 1909. In 1924, a plan was in the works to build a new campus on level land nearby, with a Gothic-style building that would reach to the sky. Here is how University of Pittsburgh chancellor John Bowman described it in announcing the project at a dinner at the University Club on November 6:

Pittsburgh is known as a center of wealth and of industry. It is known for the making of steel, glass, aluminum, and machinery. The idea of Pittsburgh's vast tonnage is in the minds of millions of people here and over the country. But tonnage is only one phase of Pittsburgh. There is a way of thinking here, a way of doing, an inward spirit and imagination. Out of things of the spirit, of imagination, the tonnage has come.

    The new building is to express that spirit of achievement with such force and sublimity that the whole world will understand. The building is high. It is not high, though, just for the sake of being high. It is only with height that stones can talk the language of courage and sublimity. Such a building belongs in Pittsburgh.

Dr. Frank Conrad, Westinghouse engineer (shown in his laboratory about 1921) began experimenting with "wireless telephone" in 1916. This led to amateur station 8XK in a garage behind his Wilkinsburg home. Thus KDKA had its birth. (Westinghouse Electric Corporation.)

In the 1920s, Will Rogers and Ziegfield Follies cast members team up for a special broadcast from KDKA's first downtown studio, located in the Pittsburgh Post offices at Wood Street and Liberty Avenue. On November 2, 1920, about 1,000 Pittsburghers tuned crystal sets to KDKA, based in East Pittsburgh, to hear returns of the Harding-Cox election, as furnished by telephone by the *Post*. That was the world's first scheduled radio broadcast. (Westinghouse Electric Corporation.)

Thousands of admirers swarmed into Pitt Stadium on August 3, 1927, to welcome the hero of the day, Charles A. Lindbergh. To the left of Lindbergh is Mayor Charles Kline. At far left is police superintendent Peter P. Walsh; second from right is Pittsburgh City Council president Daniel Winters. Virginia Pierce and Lucille Munn are the women in sashes. (Bert Winters.)

Frick Acres in Oakland, a gift from the Mellons, became the site of the University of Pittsburgh's new campus in the 1920s. The focal point would be the "Cathedral of Learning," a neo-Gothic skyscraper designed by Charles Klauder. (University of Pittsburgh Press.)

The $6 million Liberty Tubes project was completed in 1924; four years later, on March 27, 1928, county commissioner Joseph G. Armstrong's two grandsons undid a ribbon to open the companion Liberty Bridge. For the next 90 minutes, automobiles four abreast streamed across it, with three lanes heading into the tubes and along South Hills streets and roads lined with thousands of residents.

A sign on a house at 1711 Liberty Avenue read, "John Kane, House Painter." Also a miner, mill worker, and laborer, he used lunch hours to sketch Pittsburgh scenes such as the Bloomfield Bridge. At night, his bedroom was his studio where he worked in oils, pastels, and crayons. At 67, unknown, untrained, Scottish-born John Kane made his debut in the Carnegie International. Critics likened his work to that of Henri Rousseau. (Carnegie Museum of Art.)

In 1880, Andrew William Mellon became head of T. Mellon and Sons Bank. From it he and his brother, Richard B., with combined interests in coal, coke, steel, aluminum, oil, railroads, and more, developed one of the world's great financial empires around the Mellon National Bank, incorporated in 1902. Mellon later was secretary of the U.S. Treasury and ambassador to England; his greatest legacy is the National Gallery of Art in Washington, D.C., which owns this portrait by Oswald Birley.

Andrew William and Richard Beatty Mellon established Mellon Institute for Industrial Research in 1913. Later they supplied nearly $10 million for a new building at Fifth and Bellefield Avenues designed by Janssen and Cocken and inspired by the Parthenon. In 1932, the first of 62 columns, each weighing 60 tons, was transported to the site. (Mellon Institute.)

A depression village in the early 1930s sprang up between Penn and Liberty Avenues, extending from Seventeenth Street nearly to Eleventh Street. Next to it was old St. Patrick Church, parish of Rev. James R. Cox. From there, a jobless army of 15,000 men, under Father Cox's command, marched to Washington in January 1932 to appeal to Pres. Herbert Hoover for relief. On return, Father Cox declared himself "Jobless Party" candidate for president. (Brady W. Stewart.)

At 12:01 a.m. on April 7, 1933, thirsty Pittsburghers began drinking in a new era of brewed conviviality. In barrooms everywhere, depression gloom was put to flight as legalized 3.2 beer was gulped down in great quantities. This scene was at Louis Americus's Oyster Bar in the Diamond (now Market Square), a saloon of the brass-cuspidor, swinging-door vintage that managed to survive Prohibition. (Louis Americus.)

McKeesport's Henrietta Leaver won the Miss America crown in 1935 and later posed in a bathing suit for Italian-born Pittsburgh sculptor Frank Vittor. But the resulting statue was nude; although Leaver protested, Vittor refused to add a swimsuit. After a jury decided it was a "true and beautiful work of art," Leaver withdrew her objections. She married and retired from public life; Vittor designed more than 50 memorials and fountains in western Pennsylvania. (William Rimmel.)

On November 8, 1936, Westinghouse announced a new experimental project that it hoped would solve "much of the mystery surrounding the structure of matter." The following year the world's first industrial atom-smasher appeared in Forest Hills. There Dr. William E. Shoupp headed research leading to the discovery of photofission, the first use of gamma rays to split uranium atoms.

On March 18, 1936, streets in the Triangle lay under a sea of water, in some places 20 feet deep. Transportation was by rowboat or canoe. This was Fifth Avenue at Market Street, looking toward the Jenkins Arcade. Between 1854 and the St. Patrick's Day flood of 1936, the three rivers had risen to flood stage 112 times. (John R. Shrader.)

In 1933 Pittsburgh elected its first Democratic mayor, the erratic, controversial, and conservative William McNair. "A born windmill tilter," *Time* magazine called him, and with his resignation in 1936, newsmen sorely missed his page 1 antics. A "chief mourner" was *Post-Gazette* cartoonist Cy Hungerford, whose editorial cartoons began appearing in the *Sun* in 1914 and continued in the *Post-Gazette* after the 1927 newspaper mergers.

Eight

ANOTHER WORLD WAR AND A RENAISSANCE
1940–1959

In the early 1940s, Pittsburgh geared up to fight another war, with mills expanding and working around the clock to produce 95 million tons of steel. Even the H. J. Heinz food plant made room for a secret, emergency project where women made wings for gliders that carried troops. When the war was over, Pittsburgh looked tired, dirty, and grim. Here is how Robert C. Alberts described it in his 1980 book, *The Shaping of the Point*:

> The Point itself had never been in so low a condition. The riverbanks in places were littered with debris. Fifteen acres of freight yards and terminal and a half mile of elevated tracks were still there, largely unused. The abandoned marble Wabash Station, a 1904 vestige of the Goulds' unfortunate dream of power and profits, was being used as a government warehouse for commodities. There were vacant lots. There were a few rooming houses, some of which had been speakeasies in the Prohibition years and some of which were now places where, in the words of one observer, male patrons made short visits. There were some shops, a run-down twelve-story hotel, a good Professional Building, a residence converted to a women's club, an exclusive men's club that had been taken over as a lodge for the Elks. It was, in sum, a blighted area.

Pres. Franklin D. Roosevelt came to town on October 11, 1940, to inspect the Homestead Works and Mesta Machine plant, both important producers of war armament, and to dedicate Terrace Village, then the nation's second-largest public housing project. With him, as he was driven through streets lined with cheering crowds, were Mayor Cornelius D. Scully (center), a pioneer advocate of low-rent housing, and Sen. Joseph Guffey.

Pittsburgh was again a key shipbuilding center in World War II. LSTs (tank-landing ships, including the U.S. Navy's first) and other seagoing vessels by the hundreds slid into the Ohio River from the Dravo Corporation's Neville Island Yard. On Memorial Day 1944, LST-750, financed entirely by $5 million worth of extra war bonds bought by Allegheny County residents, was launched before a crowd of 25,000 people. (Dravo Corporation.)

Of some 192,000 men and women in the armed forces from Allegheny County, roughly 5,800 had given their lives. Among its 4,000 industries, the Pittsburgh district had produced $19 billion worth of munitions and war goods and 95 million tons of steel for wartime use, about one-fourth of the nation's total.

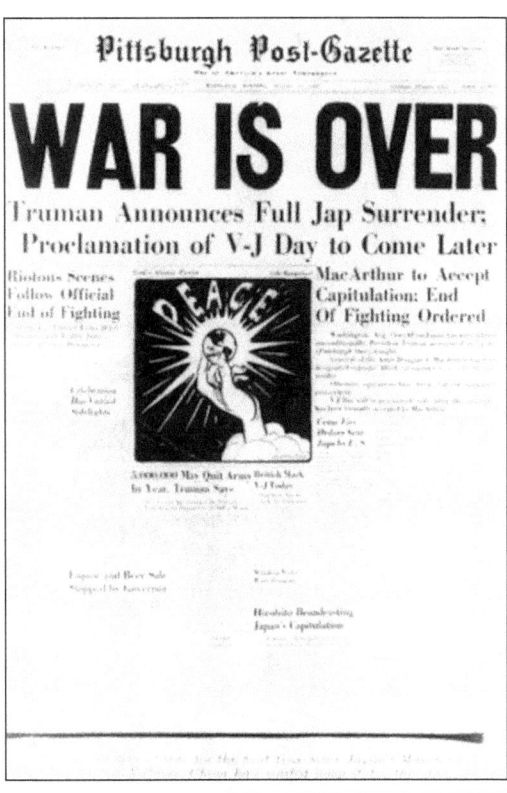

War's end brought crowds of soldiers, sailors, and civilians into streets littered with confetti. The sweet din of blowing whistles, tooting horns, and popping firecrackers filled the air, and outside the Hotel Henry on Fifth Avenue at Smithfield Street, Dorothy Nesbitt sang songs from a Jeep. This scene of jubilant abandon was on Fifth Avenue.

When the long-awaited news reached Pittsburgh at 7:02 p.m. on August 14, 1945, downtown streets were empty. "Suddenly," wrote reporter Ingrid Jewell, "they brimmed with the screaming, rushing exultant crowd." Fifth Avenue, as seen from the Smithfield Street corner with Kaufmann's clock in the foreground, was a solid mass of people. (James W. Ross.)

Hard times, floods, and four years of war had worn the luster from the Golden Triangle. Here is the Point in 1945—an ungainly, congested assortment of railroad trestles, freight yards, warehouses, manufacturing businesses, taverns, and rooming houses. The buildings at right were those of the exposition; when that annual event ceased in 1916, the main building became a skating palace, later the city automobile pound. (J&L Steel Corporation.)

Before antismoke laws began clearing the skies on October 1, 1946, it was not uncommon for Pittsburgh to be shrouded in darkness at 9:20 in the morning, when this scene was recorded at Liberty and Oliver Avenues in 1946. (George Ruark.)

In his first year in office, a rash of utility, hotel, trolley, and other strikes plagued the city, and Mayor David L. Lawrence often was on a round-the-clock schedule trying to settle them. At the peak of the 27-day power shutdown in the fall of 1946, *Post-Gazette* photographer Morris Berman caught the mayor napping at his desk in a moment of fatigue.

On November 23, 1950, the *Pittsburgh Post-Gazette*, *Press*, and *Sun-Telegraph* reported "snow flurries" were on the way. The next day they failed to publish. Pittsburgh was in snow up to its car tops—30.5 inches had fallen, the heaviest in local history. Five thousand stranded cars blocked trolley routes; National Guardsmen came in to patrol streets. On Shady Avenue, the No. 60–East Liberty trolley was an icicle on wheels. (Clyde Hare, Pittsburgh Photographic Library.)

Here is the Spring Hill neighborhood as seen by photographer Clyde Hare from neighboring Troy Hill in 1951. Many Pittsburgh hillside houses have one or two stories facing the street and three or four in the rear. In the 1950s, the population was shifting to new housing in suburbs such as Penn Hills, below.

After Greater Pittsburgh Airport opened on May 31, 1952, many families took their children to watch arrivals and take-offs from its observation decks. Inside, one of the features of the distinctive International Style terminal building was a terrazzo compass in the lobby. Another was a mobile Alexander Calder created for the 1958 Carnegie International. It now hangs in the new Pittsburgh International Airport's Airside Terminal. (Morris Berman.)

Not all of the Point was a tangle of warehouses and rail lines. Here is Penn Avenue before Gateway Center, looking toward the Point from Stanwix Street. At 425, in the days when Penn was a fashionable residential street, stood John Shoenberger's mansion, home to the city's first major art collection. In 1883, it became the Pittsburgh Club, and years later an Elks Club. It was demolished in 1950–1951. (John R. Shrader for Allegheny Conference on Community Development.)

Through ruins at the Point, the camera focuses on the stainless steel of Equitable Life's Gateway Center, the city's first downtown redevelopment project. Everywhere in 1952–1954 were the shells of old buildings going down and the skeletons of new ones rising. The *Christian Science Monitor* viewed the Golden Triangle as a "ready symbol of the new city's stirring hope in a depressed people like the V-for-Victory sign." (James P. Blair, Pittsburgh Photographic Library.)

Richard King Mellon was the man who stood behind Renaissance I, as it later became known. He began his Mellon Bank career as messenger and rose to president in 1934 at 35. From his father he learned to "live where you work and work where you live." (T. Mellon and Sons.)

Mellon Square Park came from an innovative public-private alliance—that between Richard K. Mellon's world of high finance and industry and David L. Lawrence's world of government and politics. On October 18, 1955, about 5,000 people gathered on the terrazzo plaza to watch the two men join in dedicating the park—made possible, along with its underground parking garage, through a Mellon family gift.

William Steinberg left Germany with Adolf Hitler's rise. In 1937, after helping to form the Israeli Philharmonic, he was named associate conductor of Toscanini's NBC Symphony. In 1952, he became the Pittsburgh Symphony Orchestra's permanent conductor. Under Steinberg's baton, the orchestra developed into one of the world's best and a cultural force in the community, with children's concerts, recordings, and the playing of new music. (Benjamin Spiegel.)

Founded in 1897 to aid immigrants settling in the Hill District, the Irene Kaufmann Settlement was named in memory of Henry Kaufmann's daughter when he provided a new building in 1909 at 1835 Centre Avenue, where Hill House now stands. Here is a children's class in painting in June 1950. (Esther Bubley, Pittsburgh Photographic Library.)

The Lower Hill before redevelopment, above, in 1949, was a dense mixture of well-kept homes, businesses, churches, and synagogues, as well as crowded slums overrun with rats. In the next few years most of it was swept away—95 acres cleared of about 1,300 structures, housing 8,000 people, for an all-purpose arena and civic-sports center with luxury apartment towers, seen below as envisioned in 1959.

The $22.5 million Civic Arena takes shape in April 1960. Funded in part by department store owner Edgar J. Kaufmann and designed by Mitchell and Ritchey, it featured the world's largest retractable dome. Pittsburghers weighed in on what to call it: the Auditoridome, the Big Beanie, and the Renasaucer. Civic Auditorium was its official name, but most people called it the Civic Arena—the name that fit better on road signs and so was adopted. (Howard Moyer.)

On Linton Street in the Hill District, an Urban Youth Action crew sweeps the gutter. In September 1966, neighborhood boys were involved in clean-up crews every Saturday in the Hill District.

In 1956, baker Ahmet Husseyin made flatbread in a Hill District oven. The floor of the gas-fired oven contained a one-foot-thick layer of salt to help flavor the bread.

In the 1950s, John H. Moreland, then in his 70s, tended vegetable gardens on a vacant lot at the corner of Shomin and Hazel Streets, a site later occupied by St. Francis Central Hospital, which was demolished in March 2008 to build a new Penguins arena. To grow tomatoes, cabbage, lettuce, and turnip greens, he cleared ashes and trash from the lot and surrounded each garden plot with a fence of salvaged lumber and wire.

Dr. Jonas Salk prepares to draw blood from Arthur Donahoo of Washington, Pennsylvania, as part of vaccine testing to combat infantile paralysis in the early 1950s. From his University of Pittsburgh laboratory came a polio vaccine; in 1954, Dr. Salk personally began the first inoculations to 137 children at Arsenal School in Lawrenceville. On April 25, 1955, mass immunization started.

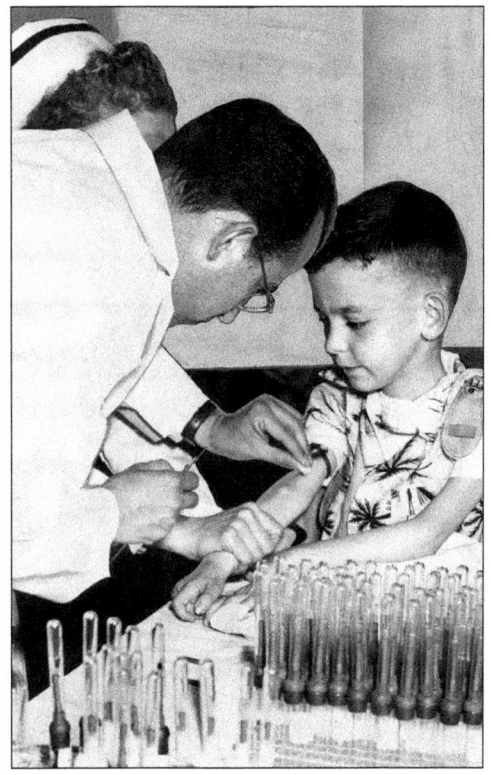

In the 1950–1958 period, the University of Pittsburgh expended nearly $35 million on seven major new buildings, bought more than $12 million worth of real estate, and initiated a master plan for an integrated campus with six to eight more new buildings. Its prime sources of strength: Mellon family foundations, with more than $40 million in gifts, and Alan M. Scaife, trustees' chairman until his death in 1958. (Clyde Hare.)

Soviet premier Nikita Krushchev, who spent 13 days in the United States in 1959, visited the Mesta Machine plant in West Homestead on September 24. Three days later, in a nationally televised speech, Krushchev predicted the volume of Soviet industry would surpass that of the United States in a dozen years.

On May 26, 1959, Harvey Haddix became the first pitcher in baseball history to throw 12 perfect innings—before being beaten by a double off the bat of Joe Alcock, Milwaukee Braves first baseman, in the 13th inning.

Nine
CIVIL UNREST AND TITLE TEAMS
1960–1979

In the 1960s, the Vietnam War and the death of Rev. Martin Luther King Jr. brought tumult to dozens of American cities, including Pittsburgh. By the 1970s, the city could celebrate its professional sports teams and a new identity: the Steel City and the Smoky City had become the City of Champions. One of the champions was Pirates right-fielder Roberto Clemente, "who played the game of baseball with great passion," said his friend and fellow Pirate Manny Sanguillen. "That passion could only be matched by his unrelenting commitment to make a difference in the lives of the less fortunate and those in need. People saw Clemente as a great ballplayer and humanitarian. He was also a great father, husband, teammate, and friend." Here is how Clemente saw it: "Any time you have an opportunity to make a difference in this world and you don't, then you are wasting your time on Earth."

An ecstatic Bill Mazeroski heads for home plate after his 1960 World Series–winning home run against Ralph Terry and the New York Yankees. In April 2008, 57,125 fans voted the bottom-of-the-ninth homer the greatest moment in Pittsburgh sports history. (James Klingensmith.)

John F. Kennedy made the last of his six political visits here on October 12, 1962, addressing about 8,300 people at the Pitt Field House on behalf of Democratic candidates. He discarded his prepared remarks to blast away at Republicans. Some 300,000 people saw him pass in an open car en route from the airport a year before he was assassinated in Dallas. (Pittsburgh Post-Gazette.)

I. W. Abel (left) is handed the gavel as president of the United Steelworkers by David J. McDonald, the man he ousted from the post in the closely contested 1965 election. The Experimental Negotiating Agreement that Abel introduced in 1973, in which the union agreed not to strike during contract talks, revolutionized collective bargaining in the steel industry. He also worked to improve workplace health and safety and guarantee pensions. (Pittsburgh Post-Gazette.)

On September 9, 1974, the day after he pardoned Pres. Richard M. Nixon for his role in the cover-up of the Watergate break-in, Pres. Gerald Ford made a commitment to federal aid for day-to-day operations of financially troubled transit systems at a conference at the Hilton. Here he moves through a crowd into the hotel. (Pittsburgh Post-Gazette.)

Rioting in the Hill District and other neighborhoods in April 1968 following the slaying of Dr. Martin Luther King Jr. resulted in 505 fires; the death of a woman in Homestead; millions in thefts, trade losses, police, and National Guard costs; $620,000 in property damage; and 926 arrests. This is 1706 Centre Avenue after looters raided a shop selling women's and children's clothing. (Edward A. Frank.)

Just before midnight in early April, National Guardsmen keep watch over Centre Avenue. (Kent Badger.)

Born in 1907 in the Allegheny River town of Springdale, Rachel Carson grew up in a rural setting and with a mother who nurtured her love of nature. Writer, scientist, and ecologist, Carson alerted the world to the dangers of pesticide misuse and began the modern environmental movement with her 1962 book, *Silent Spring*. She graduated in 1929 from Pennsylvania College for Women (Chatham University) and three years later received her master's degree in zoology from Johns Hopkins University. In 1936, she began a 15-year career as a scientist and editor for the federal government, eventually becoming head of publications for the U.S. Fish and Wildlife Service. Carson translated her government research into popular books, including three in the 1940s and 1950s that form a biography of the ocean. One of them, *The Sea Around Us*, was a best seller for 89 weeks and by 1962 had been published in 30 languages. Carson died in 1964; today the Rachel Carson Homestead Association interprets her life and work at her childhood home.

Jazz pianist Walt Harper helped breathe life back into the Market Square nocturnal scene with the opening in June 1969 of his Attic nightclub. Harper grew up in a musical family in Schenley Heights and was a mainstay at the Crawford Grill before opening his own club. After the Attic closed in 1976, he ran Harper's Jazz Club in One Oxford Centre in the 1980s. Both clubs featured top jazz stars such as Dizzy Gillespie, Wynton Marsalis, Carmen McCrae, and Lionel Hampton.

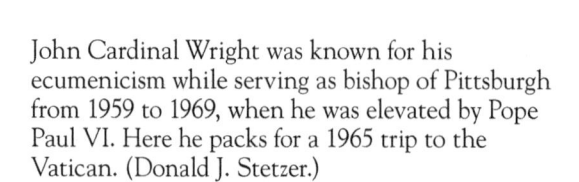

John Cardinal Wright was known for his ecumenicism while serving as bishop of Pittsburgh from 1959 to 1969, when he was elevated by Pope Paul VI. Here he packs for a 1965 trip to the Vatican. (Donald J. Stetzer.)

Sr. Jane Scully, president of Carlow College from 1967 to 1982, became the first woman elected to the board of directors of Gulf Oil Corporation in 1975. During her tenure, the college, now a university, changed its name from Mount Mercy to Carlow, honoring the Irish county the Sisters of Mercy emigrated from in 1843. (Bill Levis.)

Former U.S. Army chief of staff Gen. Matthew B. Ridgway, who led American forces in Europe and Asia, chaired the board of Mellon Institute for five years before retiring in 1960. He is shown in 1989; he died in 1993 at age 98 at his Fox Chapel home. (Bill Levis.)

The new East Liberty pedestrian mall, with fountains and pagoda-covered seating areas, wasdedicated in June 1968. To create the mall, streets were closed to cars and narrowed to create wide sidewalks that, after the dedication, proved unnecessary: shoppers stayed home in droves. (Tony Kaminski.)

This is Highland Avenue from the corner of Penn Avenue in February 1969. Three decades later, the streets were widened and parking was restored. (Morris Berman.)

After the passing of David L. Lawrence on November 21, 1966, and Richard King Mellon on June 5, 1970, new leaders emerged in various sectors, with the political arena dominated by Mayor Peter Flaherty, shown here reviewing the St. Patrick's Day parade in 1971. Frequently embroiled in feuds and controversy, Flaherty made austerity the watchword of his administration and managed to avoid tax increases during his first five years in office.

In May 1971, protesters stage an antiwar demonstration in Market Square. (Tony Kaminski.)

Tropical Storm Agnes struck the Pittsburgh area in June 1972. After four days of heavy rain, the rivers crested at 35.82 feet at the confluence—more than 10 feet above flood stage and the highest level since 1942. Point State Park was inundated, and many low-lying communities flooded. Damage was estimated at $45 million and would have been much higher but for the effective system of reservoirs and dams erected in the Monongahela and Allegheny Rivers after the flood of 1936. (Tony Kaminski.)

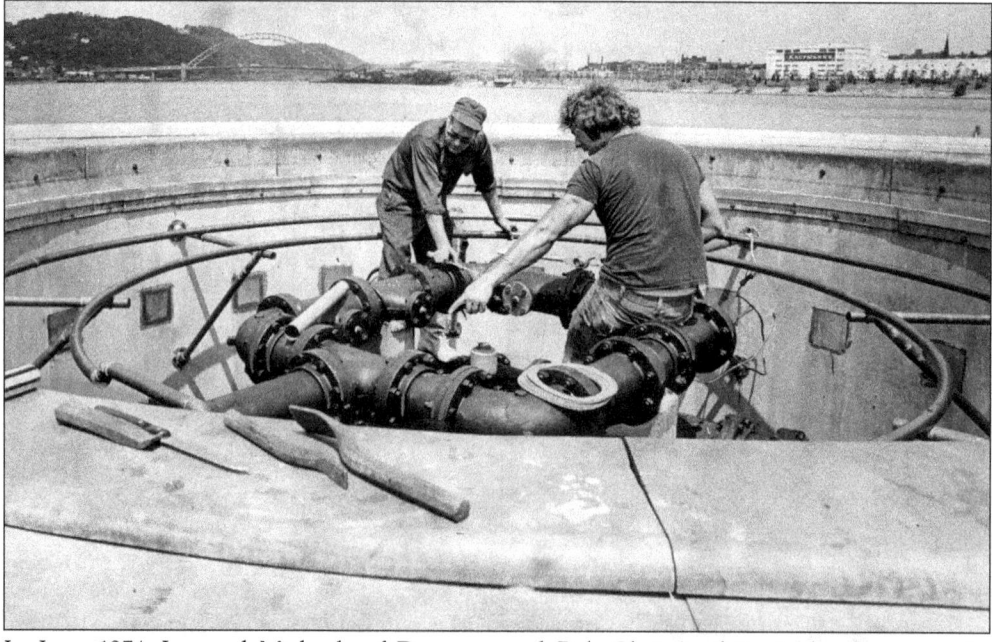

In June 1974, Leonard Michaels of Dormont and Bob Christy of Sewickley fine-tune the mechanics of the fountain that will be the new symbol of Pittsburgh. (Andy Starnes.)

Dedicated in August 1974, the fountain, with its soaring 150-foot spray, was the final component of Point State Park, which incorporated a new Fort Pitt Museum in the re-created Monongahela Bastion of Fort Pitt and the outline, in Belgian block, of Fort Duquesne in the grass.

The Pittsburgh Symphony Orchestra and other arts groups found a new home in 1971 when the Loew's Penn Theatre was converted into Heinz Hall for the Performing Arts, a glittering palace of crystal chandeliers; white, gold-leafed Corinthian columns; and crimson carpet. This image is from 1981. (Darrell Sapp.)

In the 1950s and early 1960s, the city had targeted the Mexican War Streets and five other historic North Side neighborhoods for demolition, sparking Arthur P. Ziegler Jr. and James D. Van Trump to organize the Pittsburgh History and Landmarks Foundation in 1964. The nonprofit group worked with the city to save the neighborhoods by establishing a revolving loan fund for purchase and restoration with a $100,000 grant from the Sarah Scaife Foundation.

During the gas shortage in March 1974, a sign beckons northbound motorists to the pumps of Essey's gas station in Forward Township. The oil crisis began in 1973, when members of the Organization of Arab Petroleum Exporting Companies announced they would no longer ship oil to countries that supported Israel in its war against Syria and Egypt. (Harry Coughanour, Pittsburgh Post-Gazette.)

The numbers game went legal in March 1977. On the first day of operation of the state lottery's new game, the Daily Number, players line up outside the New Diamond Market in Market Square.

Steve Blass's pitching led the Pirates to an upset World Series win against the Baltimore Orioles in 1971. In two games he quieted the Baltimore bats, limiting their powerful lineup to one run in each game. Blass became a color commentator for the Pirates in 1983.

Bruce Davenport of West View, in the striped shirt, dances in a rain of confetti during the victory celebration. (Morris Berman.)

Roberto Clemente doffs his cap to applauding fans at Three Rivers Stadium on September 30, 1973, after becoming only the 11th player in baseball history to make 3,000 hits. In less than a year he was dead at the age of 38, killed in the crash of a cargo plane off San Juan, Puerto Rico. He was bringing relief supplies to survivors of an earthquake in Nicaragua. During his 18-year career with the Pirates, he compiled a .318 lifetime batting average; his death drew attention to his other achievements as a humanitarian. (Morris Berman.)

Johnny Majors was hired away from Ohio State University in December 1972 as head football coach by the University of Pittsburgh after the Panthers had suffered a dismal 1 and 10 season, posted a 6-5-1 record in his first season, and won an invitation to the Fiesta Bowl. With him, at left in 1976, is the player most responsible for the quick turnaround, tailback Tony Dorsett, who became the first freshman to be selected All-America in 29 years.

The Pittsburgh Triangles and World Team Tennis came to the Civic Arena in 1974, with Australia native and Wimbledon champion Evonne Goolagong Cawley as the main attraction. The team won the championship Bancroft Cup in 1975, but in 1976, owner Frank Fuhrer dissolved the Triangles, and two years later the league folded.

Steeler Dwight White, with Jack Lambert (58) moving in, stops the Vikings' Dave Osborn (41) for a five-yard loss in the second quarter of Super Bowl IX in 1975. The Steelers went on to win it, 16-6. (Al Hermann.)

108

With the Steelers' victory, 42 years of patient waiting for a championship came to an end for owner Art Rooney, shown here in 1982. (Pittsburgh Post-Gazette.)

The mayhem on the gridiron could hardly match the celebration downtown that immediately followed the Steelers' triumph. Thirty-nine people were injured, and 233 arrests were made before police could restore order. When the team returned from New Orleans the next day, some 120,000 fans obliterated the motorcade route, swarming about coach Chuck Noll and his stalwarts. (Bill Levis.)

In February 1979, Veronica and Dan Marino look on as their son signs a letter of intent to play for the University of Pittsburgh. A star at Central Catholic, Daniel Constantine Marino Jr. became the Panthers' most heralded recruit since Tony Dorsett and a Miami Dolphins quarterback for 17 seasons, from 1983 to 1999. (Edwin Morgan.)

Pittsburgh again tangled with Baltimore in the 1979 series. Here the Orioles' Doug DeCinces is out at the beginning of a double play initiated by second baseman Phil Garner. Under the "we are family" leadership of coach Chuck Tanner and team captain and first baseman Willie Stargell, Pittsburgh won the championship in seven games.

Ten

BIG STEEL FALLS, HIGH-TECH RISES
1980–2008

Between 1974 and 2002, the Pittsburgh region lost more than 75,000 steel jobs. On riverfront land where the mills had stood, on the South Side, in Hazelwood and Homestead, came new communities of homes, shops, restaurants, and high-tech businesses, along with new recreational opportunities. The city's hardworking rivers, trafficked through the centuries by flatboats, keelboats, steamboats, motorboats, tugs, tows, and coal barges, now also made room for kayaks, canoes, and sculls. Alongside the rivers, railroad beds were converted to bicycle trails. In the city proper, three-term mayor Tom Murphy helped lead the transformation of the economy with several billion dollars in economic development, including new playing fields for the Pirates and Steelers and a new riverfront convention center, the largest green building in the country. Pittsburgh also became home to a museum devoted to the life and work of native son Andy Warhol, master of the innocuous bon mot, including this one: "People need to be made more aware of the need to work at learning how to live because life is so quick and sometimes it goes away too quickly."

On August 1, 1988, Dorothy Six, one of the world's biggest, most modern blast furnaces, comes to a deliberate, crashing end in Duquesne. Ultimately, failure to modernize, foreign imports, and comparatively high labor costs all contributed to the decline of the American steel industry.

Pittsburghers bade a fond farewell to the Pirates' leading home run hitter of the 1970s when Willie Stargell retired in October 1982. A hall of fame outfielder and first baseman who played his entire 20-year career with the Pirates, Stargell was a seven-time all-star who hit 475 home runs and drove in more than 1,500 runs. "His numbers were dwarfed by his humanity," wrote *Post-Gazette* sports columnist Gene Collier after Stargell's death in April 2001.

112

Robert Ferris Prince, a great-nephew of engineer George Ferris, was a big wheel around Pittsburgh himself as a Pirates broadcaster from 1948 to 1975 and briefly again just before his death in 1985. Always the team's biggest fan, he had a penchant for giving the players nicknames—like the Dog, the Deacon, and the Quail—that made them seem like familiar fellows on the neighborhood sandlot. "We had 'em alllll the way!" Prince would intone at the end of a Pirates win, whether it was true or not.

For 35 years, Myron Cope made Steelers games crackle for fans who would turn down their televisions and turn up their radios to listen to "the ever-celebrated sand-blaster of the spoken word," as Gene Collier wrote. When the *Post-Gazette* asked readers to share their memories after his death in February 2008, the response was overwhelming. "He gave us a perfect blend of chutzpa, modesty, comedy, compassion, passion and intellect," Lon Santis wrote from Ijamsville, Maryland.

Downtown saw a skyscraper boom in the 1980s, with the addition of six towers including PPG Place, Philip Johnson and John Burgee's crystalline neo-Gothic fantasy with an austere plaza whose monumental obelisk *Post-Gazette* columnist Peter Leo dubbed "the Tomb of the Unknown Bowler." In 2002, philanthropists Henry and Elsie Hillman surrounded it with useful ornaments: an ice rink and a fountain.

One of the four Carnegie Museums, the Andy Warhol Museum opened in 1994 on the North Side, celebrating the life and work of one of America's most influential artists. Showcasing a wide range of often provocative traveling exhibits and its own substantial collection of Warhol's work, the museum is a potent cultural force in the region and beyond. Here Lloyd Wilson, a student at Warhol's alma mater, Schenley High School in Oakland, tours the museum in April 2004.

Unthinkable to many, the once mighty Homestead Works, which employed 10,000, was reduced to rubble and hauled away in 1989. There was talk of an industrial park, but what finally sprang up 10 years later was a shopping center called the Waterfront, part strip mall, part Disneyesque Main Street complete with ersatz town square. Up the hill, meanwhile, Homestead's historic Main Street, Eighth Avenue, struggled to survive.

Carnegie Mellon University professor Herbert Simon, shown here in his office in 1986, was a fixture for 52 years at the school he helped transform into a leader in computer science. His research on how people make decisions was honored with the 1978 Nobel Prize in economics, and his work with Allen Newell in the mid-1950s gained renown when they created the first "thinking machine" and launched the field of artificial intelligence. He also helped establish the school's Robotics Institute. In 2006, at its National Robotics Engineering Center in Lawrenceville, the school demonstrated how its "Crusher" vehicle, below, developed for the U.S. Army, handles difficult terrain. (Above, Jim Fetters; below, Darrell Sapp.)

Dr. Thomas Starzl, whose pioneering work as a researcher, surgeon, and teacher continues to give people around the world a second chance at life, prepares a donor liver during transplant surgery in May 1985. Starzl's work elevated perceptions of Pittsburgh as a center of frontline medical research and the highest quality of health care, University of Pittsburgh chancellor Mark Nordenberg noted when the university named one of its biomedical science towers in his honor in 2006. (John Kaplan.)

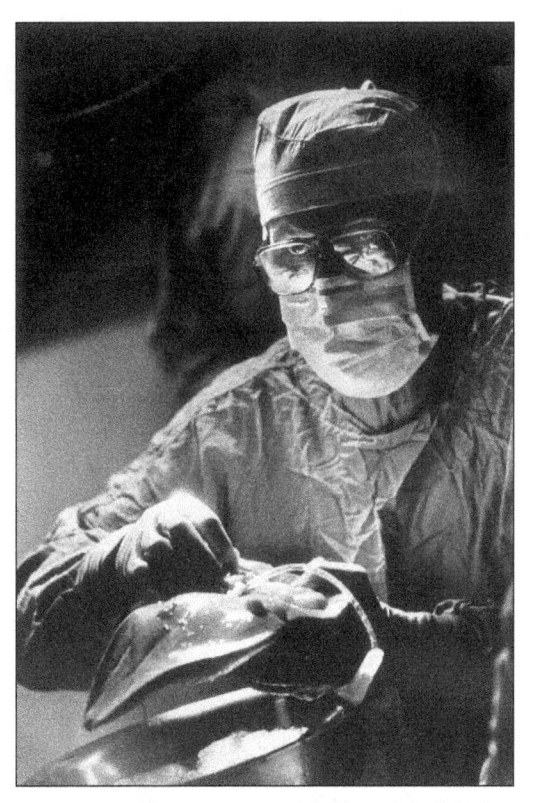

Paula Przybilinski, a carpenter with contractor P. J. Dick Corporation, signs the I-beam that will top off the new Children's Hospital of Pittsburgh in Lawrenceville in June 2006.

117

A larger-than-life Mayor Richard Caliguiri is a bronze sentinel on the steps of the City-County Building. A visionary leader and competent administrator who came up through the parks and recreation department to win a seat on Pittsburgh City Council, Caliguiri inspired the 1980s downtown building boom known as Renaissance II. With the steel industry reeling, he also launched efforts to attract high-tech industries. He was mayor from 1977 until his death from amyloidosis in 1988. (Bill Wade.)

At Caliguiri's death, Pittsburgh City Council president Sophie Masloff became the city's first female mayor. Forced to deal with a shrinking city, she successfully privatized the aviary, zoo, conservatory, and Schenley Park's golf course. She was the first to suggest that Pittsburgh build an old-fashioned ballpark for the Pirates, an idea ahead of its time. Here she conducts the Pittsburgh Symphony during the city's Fourth of July celebration in Point State Park in 1990.

On January 18, 1993, Pittsburgh Post-Gazette publisher William Block Sr. celebrates the first paper after an eight-month strike that ended with the closure of the Pittsburgh Press and the sale of its assets to the Post-Gazette.

On one of his neighborhood walks, Mayor Bob O'Connor quizzes Rayoniah Perkins about her age as he helps her out of her mother's car in Beltzhoover. A longtime city councilman, the populist O'Connor did not live to enjoy the job he had long campaigned for. He died of a brain tumor in September 2006, seven months after becoming mayor. (Bob Donaldson.)

When the Senator John Heinz History Center opened in a former ice company warehouse in the Strip District in 1996, Pittsburgh gained a large historic space in which to examine and celebrate its past. Its coglike finial, designed by Pfaffmann and Associates, pays tribute in part to the city's engineering achievements.

In June 1998, Jeannine Borelli holds her head as she listens to radio coverage of the F1 tornado that removed the third floor of her family's home on William Street on Mount Washington. It later touched down in Hazelwood, Rankin, and Donegal, Westmoreland County. The Borellis' house was torn down the next month, and they soon rebuilt. (Steve Mellon.)

Stepping into retirement in 1997, Mario Lemieux watches as his banner is raised to the ceiling of the Civic Arena. He returned to the ice in 2000 but retired again in 2006. Despite serious health problems, Lemieux battled with the Penguins for 17 seasons and became the first player to own his former team when he bought the Penguins out of bankruptcy in 1999. In 1993, the year he was successfully treated for Hodgkin's lymphoma, Lemieux created the Mario Lemieux Foundation to fund medical research. (Peter Diana.)

Jerome Bettis's final season as a Steelers running back was a Lombardi trophy winner in February 2006. "The Bus," known for his strength and nimble footwork on the field, helped drive the team to a 21-10 victory over the Seattle Seahawks in Super Bowl XL.

Suzie McConnell-Serio, born into a big Brookline family of hoopsters, competes for the Cleveland Rockers against the Washington Mystics in an August 2000 game shortly after announcing her retirement from the Rockers. She won Olympic medals in 1988 and 1992 and earned a 321-86 record as coach for 13 years at Oakland Catholic High School before coaching in the WMBA. In April 2007, she was named head women's basketball coach at Duquesne University. (Peter Diana.)

Three Rivers Stadium disappeared in a cloud of concrete dust on February 11, 2001. In its place came rugged Heinz Field and PNC Park, widely regarded as the best and most intimate traditional ballpark in Major League Baseball. Below, players line up for the national anthem on opening day in 2001. (John Beale.)

Educator, Presbyterian minister, and consummate gentleman, Fred Rogers, shown in his office in 2000, hosted *Mister Rogers' Neighborhood* for 33 years in the Oakland studios of WQED, which became the nation's first public television station when it signed on in 1954. In 2008, a memorial statue and children's park in his honor were planned for the North Shore, now home to a riverfront park and water steps, below, near PNC Park. Here Connor McAndrews, age 5, of New Kensington, makes like a fish in June 2005. (Above, John Beale; below, Robin Rombach.)

August Wilson "spent his play-writing life depicting the natural elders and shamans of his culture, in the process gradually becoming the essential, soft-spoken epitome of those elders himself," *Post-Gazette* drama critic Christopher Rawson wrote after Wilson's death in 2005. The 10 plays of his Pittsburgh Cycle—one for each decade of the 20th century—present a historical context that "speaks with passionate eloquence across the great American racial divide."

Bingo's roots go back to the Romans and a game they called lotto, but credit Pittsburgher Hugh J. Ward with refining and popularizing it in America. He ran the game at carnivals, copyrighted it, and wrote a rule book in 1933. Seventy years later, Betty Fairtrace of Plum takes her chances at the Sardis Volunteer Fire Department. (John Beale.)

125

Bicyclists and walkers stream across the Hot Metal Pedestrian Bridge on opening day in November 2007. The bridge, adapted from one that carried molten steel and other materials between Jones and Laughlin plants on both sides of the Monongahela River, now connects two sections of the 37-mile Three Rivers Heritage Trail. The bridge is a key link in the 150-mile Great Allegheny Passage between Pittsburgh and Cumberland, Maryland. (Bob Donaldson.)

In the summer of 2002, a single scull glides through the back channel of the Allegheny River at Herr's Island. Since its founding in 1984, the Three Rivers Rowing Association, with boathouses on the island and in Millvale, has given a big boost to paddling on Pittsburgh rivers. (Darrell Sapp.)

From Fiji to Florida to Fresno, California, Andrew Carnegie built 2,509 libraries between 1881 and 1917, mostly in America, the British Isles, and Canada. To this day, Carnegie's free-to-the-people libraries remain Pittsburgh's most significant cultural export, a gift that has shaped the minds and lives of millions. While many of Carnegie's hardworking steelworkers had no time for libraries, their descendants embraced them. Here, in 2008, a student is drawn to a window in the glass-floored stacks of the Carnegie Library of Pittsburgh in Oakland. (Morgan Gilbreath, Winchester Thurston.)

Guyasuta, chief of the Senecas, acted as guide to George Washington on his trip to Fort LeBoeuf in 1753, but the two soon were on opposite sides in the French and Indian War. James West's bronze sculpture, installed in 2006 on Mount Washington, depicts the reunion of the two men in 1770, when Washington came to survey lands in apparent violation of the Proclamation of 1763, which restricted white settlement west of the Alleghenies. Today the sprawling, perhaps inevitable city at their feet looks to the future as it honors its complicated past. (Samantha Wanko, Winchester Thurston.)

Visit us at
arcadiapublishing.com